RUN THE SONG

ALSO BY BEN RATLIFF

Every Song Ever: Twenty Ways to Listen in an Age of Musical Plenty
The Jazz Ear: Conversations over Music
Coltrane: The Story of a Sound
Jazz: A Critic's Guide to the 100 Most Important Recordings

RUN THE SONG

*Writing
About Running
About Listening*

Ben Ratliff

Graywolf Press

Published by Graywolf Press
212 Third Avenue North, Suite 485
Minneapolis, Minnesota 55401

www.graywolfpress.org

Published in the United States of America

ISBN 978-1-64445-328-5 (paperback)
ISBN 978-1-64445-329-2 (ebook)

2 4 6 8 9 7 5 3 1
First Graywolf Printing, 2025

Library of Congress Cataloging-in-Publication Data

Names: Ratliff, Ben, author.
Title: Run the song : writing about running about listening / Ben Ratliff.
Description: Minneapolis : Graywolf Press, 2025. | Includes
    bibliographical references.
Identifiers: LCCN 2024036043 (print) | LCCN 2024036044 (ebook) |
    ISBN 9781644453285 (trade paperback) | ISBN 9781644453292 (epub)
Subjects: LCSH: Music critics—New York State—New York (City)—
    Biography. | Music appreciation. | Music—Psychological aspects. |
    Running | Listening. | LCGFT: Autobiographies.
Classification: LCC ML423.R24 A3 2025 (print) | LCC ML423.R24
    (ebook) | DDC 780.92 [B]—dc23/eng/20240827
LC record available at https://lccn.loc.gov/2024036043
LC ebook record available at https://lccn.loc.gov/2024036044

Cover design: Kimberly Glyder

RUN THE SONG

// 1 //

Out quickly and on the move: lock the door, down the steps to the mailboxes, the front door, a courtyard, the sidewalk, the street, a crossing amid cars and buses, down the hill.

The clearest and most seductive entrance to Van Cortlandt Park, in the northwest Bronx, is on Broadway between 242nd Street and 252nd Street: the Parade Ground, the park's open mouth.

Here is a flat, green field, a mile and a half around, big enough for five or six sports events to be played on it at once—soccer, baseball, cricket in the center, cross-country running on the edges and outward into the veins of the adjacent woodlands. The volume of open sky, and the uninterrupted sound of trees and birds above, and ice, dirt, and grass underfoot, are vast by New York standards. A look across the field affords a range otherwise withheld from you in city life: you are measuring a space of which you can roughly see the outlines, and it is possible to listen toward what you hear, what you cannot quite hear, the sounds you imagine or recall, and sounds that have not yet been sounded. The air is relatively clear and relatively sweet to breathe. Light, air, sound, space.

As I look across the field from one edge to the other, I might also make this proposition: if I know a song of a sort of middle length that stays truly *on*, one worth memorizing and one that coheres, I can imagine going through all of it in my head, from beginning to end, while running one circuit of the field.

Maybe one of Jimi Hendrix's performances of "Machine Gun" from the Fillmore East on the day that 1969 turned into 1970. Maybe the fourth part of Beethoven's String Quartet no. 14, the long *andante ma non troppo e molto cantabile* section—this would take practice. Maybe Betty Carter's live version of "What a Little Moonlight Can Do" from 1982, or, if I develop really good pattern recognizing and signpost detecting, "Bhavayami" recorded in 1963 by the Carnatic singer M. S. Subbulakshmi: a devotional song glossing the entire story of the Ramayana epic. All those songs, if we can call them songs, are not *really* long, but long enough for my purpose. They don't slip past you before getting started; they have a significant body. They are long enough to take you somewhere and hover and move onward and show you something.

I am thinking of these songs because of their length, which really means their framing, created by composition and performance and, more definitively, by recording. According to their traditions, they have introductions and conclusions: at the beginning they state their case as they come into being, and to some degree they resolve at the end. And if I want to play them as individual tracks—through a streaming service, or as a digital file, or at home on a vinyl record—they are sorted with bands of silence around them so I know how to find them. Just as with a book, or a paragraph of written prose, the beginning and end of these tracks attract the most attention: they have outsize importance.

Yet each contains a deep middle, with many moments that make me wonder how I got there, moments of complicated grace when the musician's limited, everyday mind seems to vanish and I am left with that impression many might characterize as "music playing itself," or that the musicians were making up the song entirely, even making up the entire tradition that contains the song, as they go along. The perimeter is clear enough. I'd like to be in the middle.

This grace occurs in Subbulakshmi's casual blazing through her song's maze of ornamental tags and trills, the required reshuffling of emphasis in repeated lines, with the tabla player and sitarist hanging on to her lead, making the song swing and dip and flap around: few songs are so complicatedly intense. It occurs in Betty Carter's commitment to the high level of expression she seeks, as the chords of the standard tick by underneath her long vowels, as if she were putting certain words under a microscope: nearly from the start, she climbs entirely inside the dynamics of the music; she becomes sound and she pushes the other musicians forward. It occurs for sure in Hendrix, warming up his cracked-open blues scale until he begins to render a soldier's tale of his own death while the bullets are flying into him, actually singing to the gun, elongating the moment of death, and then after the soldier can no longer speak for himself, the story becomes environmental, through a guitar description of the surrounding gunfire chaos, perhaps a medevac, perhaps a funeral, or the illusion of one, and then the sound of spirits—not notes but feedback swoops and cries to create a weird sonic luminescence, letting the materials of amp and guitar become equal partners in the sound. Hendrix does all this without really resorting to narrative. It is never clear where one scene ends and the next scene begins, or if they are scenes. He is instead creating overlapping impressions, and also creating a room in which all this is happening. All these songs are perhaps better understood as places.

Hendrix does something like this in every version of the song from those Fillmore East concerts, but the versions are different on both micro and macro levels. There's not one fixed story. I've known at least one of these versions since I was young, but I didn't really hear any of it well until I started running with it at age fifty-one, first around the Parade Ground and then through the woods. Only then could my commitment to the action begin to correspond with his; only then could I stay with it as it moved along, rather than grasping bits of it as they flashed past.

Music appears not to serve a measurable vital function, like air, water, light, food, or love; if it is less than those, it is also more. Music connects people and makes them understand the limits of connection—it is a medium of communication, but more important, of play. Music involves pattern recognition, and becomes helpful in forming and delineating a self: you can use music to feel more like a certain social type, and more unlike a certain social type. It merges you and keeps you separate.

Though music has no tangible form, it has a physical form, and can enter a body. Moving with it—running with it, as I run around my neighborhood—can make it a memento or marker for a present and a past experience. Running with it can also reveal music as a disposition, as a philosophy, or as an open system, even if you don't own the music as a physical document.

Pretty soon, describing music along these lines, you will start to rely on metaphors. Unfortunately, many of the available metaphors in English have to do with vision.

A song can be a window. The window represents an opening in your closed-in perception, such that you can clearly perceive a particular subject outside yourself. The dimensions of the window might be the beginning and the end of the song, its lowest note and its highest, the points of your apprehension of it and perhaps your surrender to it, your over- and underestimation of it. Through the song-window you can "see" a distinct and particular vantage of life outside your own. Perhaps many days you pass by the window—it is just another window. One day you might really "see" through it and love the junction of light and angles so much that they become a part of you.

A song affords a "view" of another person: the person who made it. The person may sing in a language you do not understand, play an instrument and use a vocabulary of sound you know little or nothing about. Sometimes none of that matters: all that matters is that you have properly "looked" through its window, and your own life has expanded to the dimensions of what the window reveals to you.

A song is a road. Smaller now, more personal: a song is a trail. More generically: a song is a path. I am not necessarily thinking about a path between point A and point B and back to A again, as Maurice Merleau-Ponty used the idea of a "path" to define communication between two people. I am thinking more about a forward action with no particular point B, in which the movement itself, and the expansion of your life according to what you perceive while moving, becomes the whole event. Now forget the metaphors: let's call it a song again. When you listen to a song, the song is creating a new version of you, and you are creating a new version of the song.

Music *develops*. Its makers, working at their best, can't entirely know the music's outcome for itself, themselves, or you. Music is nonvisual, and if that's a limitation, it's one that helps.

Visual codes are increasingly limited and manipulative, and also too easy to limit and manipulate. The visual is efficient and facile proof of authority, a *good enough* reason for the viewer to acquiesce and stop thinking. Appearances have kept people apart; complexions create castes and wars. The aural is never quite good enough proof, but never-good-enough in a strangely hopeful way. It leaves room for doubt or a second thought. It may invite you to think more, or to attend to the thing you do not yet understand.

Music, now, this morning, on the field where I'm just starting out, establishing today's relationship to the path—I look up at the sky, down at the field, notice my feet as if they were someone else's, realize they are slightly sore around the big toes, and further realize I don't care—comes through without false messages. It seems a counterforce to the cruelty and obviousness of the world.

When I wonder what I want to take on a run, I find myself thinking, prescriptively, "Only the most careful, practiced, slowly changing music will do it for me these days," a nice enough thought, and thus the Finnish singer Cucina Povera, who works close-miked and with great care, as if you were an egg that she did not want to break. Maybe an hour later I find myself thinking, "Only the most abrupt, startling, confrontational music will do it for me these days," and thus Nosebleed, the Virginia hardcore band, whose music sounds like ripping a wound open. I'm all right with that.

There are plans to open up a two-hundred-bed FEMA field hospital at Van Cortlandt Park. I'm not quite sure what day the work started. A third of the Parade Ground has been fenced off. The local newspaper confirms the plans. There are no tents, and thus no beds, and thus no sick people, just a containment for them.

The fence goes right across the fine-gravel path encircling the field. You can't get around it; if you forget and run up to the fence, you have to reroute for five to ten minutes to get beyond the fence and out toward Broadway—provoking a properly frustrating feeling. It's almost a psychological test. I have forgotten about the fence a few times now; my mind is somewhere else. Then I get within fifty feet of it and slowly turn around, believing that surely I am the only idiot who has failed to absorb its presence. This isn't punishment fencing to keep people in; it is preservationist fencing to keep people out. I once saw this same principle at work in a Nova Scotia national park. Its purpose was described by signs. There, it was called an exclosure.

Exclosures are startling. They seem to go against the nature of things. Cells fuse to form organs and tissues in living things; living things eventually fuse with the earth. Most divisions are disputed, and most fortresses don't stay fortressed. I am wanting to run through the park, not around it, and to listen through the song, not around it.

// 2 //

William DeVaughn's "Be Thankful for What You Got": the song, and the whole album of the same name. I start it at the three-way intersection near home, running in place as I do out of superstition and while waiting for the sparse traffic to clear, wanting to hear the sound of the record without thinking of the lyrics, or even of the title of the song, and I laugh through my mask—a bandanna—when its message sinks in.

The song comes from the flash years of Philadelphia soul when that intent, upholstered music—of strings, horns, vibraphones, electric pianos or organs, alert drumming, and singers' calls for consolation and respect—built a standard of American pop music, at least on the East Coast. Those songs were among the first I came to recognize when I started listening to AM radio. But this is a scaled-down version of Philly soul—no strings, no horns—and anyway DeVaughn was a visitor to Philly soul: he worked as a civil engineering technician for the District of Columbia Water and Sewer Authority, designing infrastructure. The three-quarter-face depiction of DeVaughn on his album cover shows him in thought, holding a pencil in his left hand; he could be writing a song, but he could also be drawing a sewer. He paid for his own initial recording of "Be Thankful" with a Philadelphia producer, who then developed it further into a radio hit, DeVaughn's only one.

The message of "Be Thankful" first speaks into life car-pleasures, car-status, car-desire: a Cadillac with "gangsta whitewalls, TV antennas in the back." The brown cover of the album it appears on, that particular shade of brown, suggests a brown car from that time, 1974, maybe a Ford Gran Torino. And then the message turns, making the car not particularly special, just relative to other pleasures, another consolation among many. Magically, DeVaughn removes the object of desire: a car song about how cars are beside the point. (The line that grips you is "You may not have a car at all.")

When I run with music, I know I'll be listening for a while, without stopping, into the unforeseen future, and so I find it easy to listen in larger expanses. Considering "messages," I realize the record is full of them. The MFSB house rhythm section at Philadelphia's Sigma Sound Studios—Earl Young / Rusty Jackman / Larry Washington / Vince Montana, and the rhythm guitarist Norman Harris, with his pulsing details, little jets in the offbeats—amount to the sound of highly practiced imprecision. All of them complement and protect one another's sound. (Blood responsibility was part of the ethos of the musicians, a position greater than the sounds they made: MFSB stood for Mother, Father, Sister, Brother.) This record is, up to a point, "another record," of a type. It's not set against the market. DeVaughn's vocal performance sounds a bit derivative, particularly of Curtis Mayfield. But the protective impulse spreading through its musicianship also moves outward, which is to say it wants to take care of the listener: it instinctively does more than the minimum to instill some strength in you and help you keep moving. If we can anthropomorphize the song, in a limited way—I'm all right with it—somehow the song knows its reach will be limited, and nevertheless it is trying to reach well, because what are we here for? We imagine a future and make efforts to reach it. DeVaughn's message isn't particularly religious; it sounds pre-religious. This record represents realistic goals and limited means.

Limited means might be useful for any sort of daily practice. In a daily practice you might as well be satisfied with who you are each day, because who you are is really all you have—or, rather, the degree to which you recognize your ongoingness is all you have. I stretch for fifteen minutes and go. I'd prefer that the equipment didn't matter. Twice a year, I buy a new pair of training shoes made by a US company, whose colors are a shame. (Lucky are the sprinters, who get to wear bright, vivid colors.) I run with neutral movements—meaning that at some point after the normal sideways roll of the striking foot, the whole width of my forefoot comes in full contact with the ground—and switch between two different types of shoes for neutral runners. I wear socks until they rip. Generally, I keep only two of everything else: shorts, long pants, jackets. I use earphones made by a Danish company, which I like mostly because I know they won't fall out of me, and a Velcro arm-holster thing for my phone. I could carry music more easily through a special watch that could also measure other physical data, but I don't want a watch for that. I don't want to know the data. I'd rather be inefficient while checking in with the ongoingness. The acknowledgment of my ongoingness should be unclocked and inefficient—lest it turn, somehow, into an optimizing force, or worse yet, an acknowledgment of my uniqueness. Listening might help. After all, listening is the opposite of holding forth on one's uniqueness.

But listening is not passive. What's passive is the subset of hearing that could be called dishearkening, the kind of thing a lot of people do around music designed for backgrounds. Here's what I figure: if you are ready to really listen to William DeVaughn—to really listen in a way that perhaps you have not done before, to his intent, to what he implied as well as to what he sang—then you are far more likely to also be listening to your own expanded present, a present with some past and some future.

And so as I move forward around the field, I work with DeVaughn's music by putting my own sensibility next to it, or by working in its gaps, or by responding in kind. I persist, moving at a medium pace, trying to remember who I am and what my limitations are—I don't train, I don't race, I don't run marathons, I can't be twenty again—and mostly trying to feel whole. (Patience and highly practiced imprecision, I remind myself, like MFSB.)

Certain words and phrases unusual in their everydayness pop out as the record continues. "Hold On to Love" is the only soul song I can think of that contains the word "depressed." It suggests that you not give up. (DeVaughn gives you this encouragement: "Hold on, hold on, hold on, hold on, hold on, hold on, hold on, hold on, because *tomorrow just might be the day.*") Ultimately, he doesn't need to win, because there is a tomorrow, and tomorrow is bigger than his song.

I run every day to feel whole: Do I listen every day for the same reason? If I don't, my body aches, my brain is overfull, I lose track of who I am, and I live by rote. It's a daily practice, but it's also self-preservation.

"Listening," wrote my friend Harmony Holiday, "knowing one another by sound and voice, is the first law of black liberation—

without this skill there is no self-preservation." Her definition suggests what the musicologist Judith Becker might have called Harmony's "habitus of listening." Becker, writing in the early 2000s, borrowed the term "habitus" from the sociologist Pierre Bourdieu. She argued that everyone's listening is a result of factors that are probably outside their control; that most people are part of a "community of interpretation," whether they know it or not; that many of us think we're the captain of our ship when we're listening, just us and our tunes, but no, there's always more to it. Becker encouraged us to consider that listeners settle into a certain kind of aural "gaze," the same way people talk about "the male gaze" (Becker is not the only writer who laments the lack of an equivalent listening word for "gaze"), et cetera, and she supposed this gaze-of-listening might be partly determined by one's family history, class, locale, values, work, social traditions, and deeper on down the line into the ways of a people.

Within my own habitus of listening, recognition, self-preservation, and liberation don't have the same implications as they do for my friend. I recognize the world through listening; I also self-preserve and seek a kind of liberation. But because of my own background, and because I became a journalist and critic, I do certain other things. I also still presume a bit of independence, as many of us journalists and critics do, that Becker might find amusing.

That independence—the notion that I can stand at a neutral remove from music, and that a piece of music can be considered somewhat free from the conditions that made it—started at some point to trouble me. The trouble hasn't stopped. Paradoxically, I am also troubled by the notion that any thorough habitus of listening may require an autobiography, or a thorough explanation of the conditions that made me. Memoirs by critics in book form constitute a tortured genre. A habitus carries a promise of context beyond one's own standpoint; autobiography does not. Yet all writers offer privileged information to readers—their writing is determined by what they want and don't want to offer, what they want to reveal and what they want to conceal. My concern is: Can I write about listening without reverting to a life story?

○

What sort of listener am I?

Here is a crack at my habitus of listening. An isolated, suburban Hudson Valley, 1970s, slow-time-passing, AM radio into free-form FM radio, White, upper-middle-class, atheist, uprooted, art-and-politics, newspaper- and novel-reading household attuned to signs and facts. My father grew up in Ohio, moved to New York in 1955 for art school, and eventually worked as a graphic designer within the Manhattan visual-art world, translating the intent of an artist or a gallery into arrangements of texts and images for exhibition catalogs, posters, advertisements in newspapers and magazines, and books. My mother grew up in England, studied poli-sci at Oxford, and cowrote a book called *British Political Facts 1900–1960* as a research fellow there; in her American professional life, which began in 1963, she continued with facts as a fact-checker for Time-Life Books, then managed my father's office and did the bookkeeping. They were both fish out of water or birds out of air, which is likely how I learned to feel similarly.

In the part of the Hudson Valley where I grew up, there was no town square. No commuter rail; bicycle and bus instead. No walking to friends' houses, but plenty of woods. Weather and pines outdoors, records indoors. Not a lot of extended family relations; really just us. I had been born in New York City and spent my early years in England, and when we returned I had some child's version of critical distance from America and Americans; I was raised nonspiritual and suspicious of institutions, but I learned and worked in a few big ones. Possibly because I did not have much of a neighborhood—geographically, or in terms of family and family customs—I felt free to visit others. When I started listening to some of the music in our house, I sensed the workings of a neighborhood within specific records—Stevie Wonder's *Songs in the Key of Life*, *Beatles for Sale*, Camille Saint-Saëns's *The Carnival of the Animals*, the early rock and roll and doo-wop from the *American Graffiti* soundtrack, Louis Armstrong's Hot Fives—and then a nearly limitless number of other neighborhoods, adjacent or secretly connected to them. I wanted to know about all music. I dreamed of moving beyond the informed but slowed-down musical knowledge of my parents, and of hearing music (always male music, at the time) that most people didn't know about, from now or the past, while remaining close to but critically distant from the communities of that music. I became so invested in music that I worried it might make me a monster unless I betrayed it a bit, was disloyal to it. I felt wary of any club liable to induct me, even the ones near me, even New York hardcore, even New York jazz, both of them listener-clubs that valued integrity and loyalty. I was happiest with romantic partners who were not "into music."

At twenty-one I walked into a show at the Museum of Modern Art called *Fragmentation and the Single Form*: paintings, collages, ceramic tile, sculptures, and photographs selected from the museum's collection by Ellsworth Kelly, all demonstrating ways to loosen the story around a single form, ways (in Kelly's words) "for emptying shape of representational content and for projecting it into a new space." Here was a late Cézanne, some Picasso and Georges Braque paintings, a Hans Arp collage, an Edward Weston photograph, and also something that seemed to come from a different menu: a painting of a roseate tern made by John James Audubon in 1832. The big, detailed bird filled most of the picture space, angled down and to the left; you might want to say it was dive-bombing a fish, but to say that would tell a story. The tern had been cut out tightly from one sheet of paper and applied to another sheet of watercolor-blue background. Its flattened edges looked strange against the presumed round volume of sky; it was in the air and not in the air. The tern messed with my head for several reasons. Audubon, great artist and repellent man, had taken the bird out of its context just to the extent that the image was no longer easily understood as a matter of figure and ground; or had suggested a new dimension of possibilities where figure and ground were not predetermined. Surely that tern had something to do with my parents, and me, and people I was drawn to. But more to the point, it was Kelly who clarified the tern for us by taking a beautiful image of a bird for the enjoyment of those who liked birds and putting it alongside other works of art that had been generally coded as "abstract." The idea of grouping things together that were not usually grouped together eventually took hold of me as a listener even more than as someone who sometimes looked at art.

Later, via the work of writing about music four or five times a week for a newspaper, jazz and metal and hip-hop and Puerto Rican and Brazilian and African music—because that's what the news of a New York week in music was—I came to value the part of live music where "material" (the copyrightable entity) becomes neutral, and suddenly there is no explicit emphasis on beginning and end, such that one finds the ongoing middle, even better if genre or style markers become limited in use and suddenly don't have to matter: one is lost, the ground has given way, and that is where the real writing might begin.

My community of interpretation for listening had at first been a group of other roseate terns, figures with unclear relationships to the ground (usually male, some very sensitive or chaotic; a few died young). With them I spent a lot of time in record stores and sitting next to stereos and making tapes, always moving music around, sending it forward, replicating the message-in-a-bottle promise that any song carries with it when made public. Then, later, my community became those who listen for any reason—I am eager to share sound with anybody, and even prefer that they not be like me. Must get free of old clans. The imprecise and useful myth in my family was that we had no old clans. My mother was far more compassionate than her communist parents—Doris Lessing's *The Golden Notebook*, published just after she finished university, described her parents' arrogant and argumentative world somewhat—but by her moral system, nostalgia was an affliction on the order of narcissism. And so I listen to my old favorites cautiously, skeptically, although I am happily surprised by realizing which music has and hasn't become a part of me.

Otherwise, I have not lost a slightly haunted habit of wanting to listen outside myself, to get over my old assumptions— because they are always incomplete, if not wrong—and to see if I can learn to tune myself up with music that is not all-about-me. The electric fences of the habitus are snob, bore, nostalgist, narcissist. When I am these things, and I am, I must know how I am these things, and try to be them such that I can try to see the positions from the outside, as part of the habitus.

I run as a single form, a figure with an unfinished relationship to its ground, listening to Harmony's idea about listening, first on its own; then for how it explains something about what William DeVaughn might be listening for; then for how my own listening to DeVaughn might be opened up a little bit.

// 3 //

This neighborhood is only sporadically organized into grids. The roads follow the contours and terracing of the land. Their shapes, on maps of the area at the beginning of the twentieth century, suggest rickety fence posts being crushed between whorls and bell curves. It is often unclear, in this neighborhood, how far you've gone; and if you are a city runner oriented toward using numbered streets or the regular recurrence of new blocks to measure your progress, you might not be sure when you're on your way into measurable territory.

○

What sort of runner am I?

Here is a crack at my practice. Most days I run four to twelve miles. Some days I don't. I trust running completely, the way I trust listening. I don't know ahead of time what it's going to reveal to me, but it's going to reveal something to me. I've tried races, and can see their appeal, but I'm not particularly interested in them. So I don't train. Most days I run while listening to music. Likewise the practice of listening-while-running never feels connected to training; its goals aren't fixed. The violist Kim Kashkashian once told me that her best playing involves intention but not desire. Listening, at best, might begin with desire but transforms into something more like intention. It barely has goals. Goals are static, abstract, and removed from action, while listening is present and ongoing, part of one's perception and proprioception.

When music becomes oppressive, I take the earphones out.

I began running, skeptically, in 2012. A friend in Maine, who at the time was spending about half his days outdoors teaching young children, tricked me into running around a little island near his house one morning in August. I think he framed it mainly as something to do. There was no talk about it being good for us. I'm not even sure we called it running, as opposed to "going around the island."

Later that day we happened to visit the studios of Bob Ludwig, the esteemed audio-mastering engineer, who until recently worked in Portland. If you are Pharrell Williams or Steve Reich, and you have finished recording and mixing a new album, you still need a person to make authoritatively sure that the sound across the length of the album is even and coherent, and emphasizes particular frequencies in a way consistent with your intent. Bob was that person. To reward my curiosity about what proper listening conditions sound like for what he does, he sat me in a central chair within his master-control audition studio, at a triangle point about fifteen feet away from two obelisk speakers, and put on a CD without telling me what it was. It turned out to be "So What," from Miles Davis's *Kind of Blue*, a piece of music I know well and find easy to follow; it almost tells you, step by step, how to write a song.

I heard Paul Chambers's opening bass notes setting up Bill Evans's series of little paratactic piano phrases, recorded a long time ago in the grand resonance of Columbia 30th Street Studio, and then the rest of the band sneaking in. In a listening context such as Bob's studio, your expectations can become unreasonable— your heart doesn't stop, and you wonder why it doesn't—but I felt a more specific dilemma. I was aware of something in the music I knew to be there, and that I had long sensed, but that in these first-level conditions, I still wasn't getting. I wasn't quite *in* it. I was more around it, right on the perimeter. I heard its outer handsomeness and its form but not its inner strangeness. I wasn't feeling its nerves, or whatever restlessness would give someone the idea to make music as abnormal as that in the first place.

Back home, I began to run around a park in upper Manhattan, extending the idea of something-to-do. Most days I had to start thinking about my writing task from the moment I got up—my window to file a story closed at about 1 p.m.—so I felt obliged to take with me into the park whatever music I was writing about. As I ran, finding an alertness parallel to whatever I was listening to, I would form an idea of a way to start an essay, or a description of a sound as I felt it through moving limbs and whizzing atmosphere, sometimes an idea so crazy I had to dare myself to type it out. The ideas themselves felt motile, headlong, like music. Sometimes they made it all the way through my fingers, through my own revisions, through a backfield editor and a copyeditor and into print. This thrilled me in an almost vandalistic way.

A while later I asked a friend—another music person, the owner of a record label, who runs so much and with such a sense of ritual and meaning that she dedicates her marathon entries to deceased friends—how she listened while running: a phone attached to her arm, or . . . ? She answered that she only ran. No music. "I recommend it," she wrote.

I know what she means. Running in silence can be clarifying.

It is a significant break from the near-constant broadcast that may be your life. It helps to sensitize you for whatever it is you do with the rest of your day. And so I went without music for a long time. But then I started to miss the crazy feeling, and started to listen-while-running again.

When I doubted some aspects of my job in a serious way— wondering if criticism as I had learned it was doomed to be inadequate, and whether its vantage point needed a shift I couldn't easily make—running redeemed each day, and when I went through the disarray of leaving the job and building a different way to make a living, running reminded me of who I was and what I was up to. For that I suppose I could just as well have done a different kind of daily practice. The critic and novelist Amit Chaudhuri, who is also a singer in the Hindustani classical-music tradition, has written that one's own creative work can quickly seem unrecognizable after the fact, as if it had been done by someone else. He found that *riyaaz*—the singer's daily practice—is the antidote, "an intervention in the artist's feeling of discontinuity." An intervention into discontinuity is a paradox, and a paradox helps in perceiving a truth, if not a fact, and the truth here must be that running is my *riyaaz*, and will be until my knees give out. At the moment they're all right.

After the fall of 2016, I found running to be more than an act of continuity: it was a way to transform disappointment. Its headlong feeling delivered to me more than a report on who-I-am and how-I'm-feeling-today. It brought the necessary lightness to think about a near future, when that sort of imaginative path seemed limited or blocked. After March 2020, even more so. "In here" was fine, and contained most of my purpose: in here was my wife; and our sons in their last years before leaving us; and my college students, now seen fifteen at a time through a screen. "Out there," on streets and trails and former rail paths and aqueduct lines, running became the project, and I listened hungrily, as I ran, to a semblance of everything: to Pop Smoke, Charlie Parker, Johann Sebastian Bach, Gene Ammons, Deli Girls, Laurel Halo, William DeVaughn, Black Sabbath, Silvia Tarozzi, the Clark Sisters, Joni Mitchell, Erykah Badu, Chic, Loraine James, Kraftwerk . . . And, eventually, to some musicians or singers or DJs whose music suited not my running tempo but what I understood to be my terms of perceiving the world: Mal Waldron, Sade, Doris Jeane, Jimi Hendrix, Theo Parrish, Larry Harlow, Ed Blackwell.

Starting in the spring of 2020, as I ran I found I was listening really well, strangely well, better than ever. This feeling was something to trust. It occurred to me that there was a connection between the act of listening and the act of running, and I began to write from that point of connection. As I started writing, I didn't know what my work was, but it was what I was doing, and the same went for my running, and the same went for my listening. So I found a unity of purpose, or perhaps of non-purpose. I didn't want only to understand what I already thought I understood; I wanted to keep moving toward something. Whenever possible, I listened to music that friends mentioned in passing, or dance-music DJ sets, or followed inklings that occurred to me a minute before leaving the apartment—anything to help the headlong effect.

o

Music has motion. It has other things, too, but for me, it almost *is* motion. No motion, no music. The motion could be expressed through a rhythm, steady or varied, or through the connection of one tone to the next, or as the progression of a single tone into silence, or simply by the way music comes to you, as traveling sound waves moving through the air and the body. Running amplifies the motion in music. It took me a long time to understand this. Running while listening can be somewhat related to singing or playing along to music, but with a particular emphasis on moving, as all music does, as all music must do.

It is true that I am running through a physical atmosphere and sometimes close to a "natural" one—that is, not only an outdoor atmosphere, but an atmosphere not particularly developed or landscaped, an atmosphere not primarily defined by a human-made path through it. Therefore, I wonder whether listening closely to any music while running that is not the sound of my physical atmosphere is an inane superimposition. Perhaps to honor running properly is to put nothing in my ears. That is a problem. How to reckon with it?

One answer is: don't run, dance. Then you can inhabit a place, move to music in that place, and hear the sound of the music corresponding with the sound of the place. But I have a feeling that dancing doesn't quite unlock music in the way I want it to. It's as if dancing aspires to be music, but music aspires to be running.

I'm not talking about letting the music guide you toward the fantasy that you *are* a particular musician, as if it were possible to borrow the self of Playboi Carti or Martha Argerich for an hour, though these may be nice fantasies. I am also not talking about accepting the music as encouragement for running at a certain tempo, or for adhering to an exercise program. Most of the small amount of writing I have found about running-and-listening is about kinesiology and optimal physical performance—about music chosen mostly to set a pace, to fulfill a precept about motivation.

Here I'm referring to recent studies like some often-quoted ones involving the research of the English sports psychologist Costas Karageorghis. He argues that "self-selected motivational music" increases our "running economy," which means, among other things, our needing less oxygen for higher performance. "Motivational music" has more than 120 beats per minute, as well as, per one of the studies, "catchy melodies, inspiring lyrics, an association with sporting endeavour, and a bright, uplifting harmonic structure." "Self-selected" means familiar.

This book, then, is not about optimal music for running. Nor is it about optimal earphones. I am working in the area between Costas Karageorghis and my friend who knows music very well but refuses to listen to it as she runs.

I am talking about *running the song*: a way to engage with the music's forward patterns, its implications, its potential, its intention, and even its desire. As I run, the music I'm listening to presumes a setting, and the setting presumes a music, as if my feet were drawing the music in the physical world. In doing so, I allow the physical world to become more vivid. Running-while-listening through any atmosphere—say, the ten-mile radius around our apartment building in the northwest Bronx—helps me to understand and discern the way music operates in time and place. Running the Bronx and Yonkers and upper Manhattan has disclosed the city to me as far more than "streets": it is hills, dales, and curves, canting and terraced rock, marshes, forests, highways, streams, bridges, ripped wire fences, places of worship and of burial, blocked paths and invitations to connect interrupted planes. Likewise, running with music has disclosed music to me as more than the givens of notes, styles, genres. Running and listening can illuminate each other: you remain aware of your current position, while thinking about where you're heading and where you've been. It could be possible to write about running with the vocabulary of listening, and to write about listening with the vocabulary of running. You might start with the word "track." The word comes from Middle English and Middle French, *trek* and *trac*. At first it meant evidence of motion in the past, like a footprint, but then it came to mean a suggestion for motion in the future—a way forward. Its earliest known use as a noun denoting a single bounded selection of a phonograph record, and its earliest known use as a noun describing intentional or organized running, seem to have been almost concurrent: in 1904 and 1905, respectively.

Criticism is discernment about an arrangement, but neither the discernment nor the arrangement need be fixed. Running-while-listening creates the conditions for a kind of unforced criticism on the move. As I run through my city's arrangement, the music I listen to—via its own arrangements—starts to assume a place. Not necessarily the same place I am running through, but a place nonetheless. (The singer Jim Legxacy's place is tight and sharply defined, but with misty, blurry contents. The composer Laurel Halo's is open, but with divots and irregularities. The saxophonist Eric Dolphy's is eccentrically gridded and magically coordinated.) And therefore my deepest intention around music starts to become real, which is to get it into me, and to get myself into it, to embody the actions it describes, so that I may find moments of becoming it, even as it moves away from me, which it must.

So maybe there is a way to run and listen such that several things can happen. I can try to describe the motion of the music and the motion of the body, and the space of the music and the space of the body, as blurring into each other. And I can also use the headlong force of music to run among and connect entities that are for some reason not configured to be together: neighborhoods and people and time periods and traditions. Literally, this means that in a single run I can connect those who lived along the track I trace: say, Ella Fitzgerald and DMX. They knew the same land, its topography and weather and wind. In that example, the task exists for me before I put my shoes on. But the possible connection between, say, Hendrix and Subbulakshmi, who might never have walked the same ground—a connection made not only via the length of their songs, but via their alertness in bending notes as they move forward—can also be made when I'm moving forward with them.

If none of this can be proved or properly resolved, and if the irresolutions are problems, I have to be all right with these problems, and others. Such as: I am a runner, and also I might not be, because I don't train or race. I write music criticism, but in some ways I betray it, because I am wary of misconstruing it by containing it. I run with music to help me merge with the external world, but I am sometimes using it to help me define myself against it, like the tern flattened against the blue sky. (To run is to be out in the world, but also to be alone.) I move in what seems to be a history and a narrative of this place and time, and I seem to distrust history and narrative. I've been formed in every way, as a listener and a runner and a writer, by outside forces, and I also feel a subjective consciousness, as most listeners do. I generally don't like to write about myself, but a self runs and a self listens, so what can you do. As I run I am in search of a clear way to think, to manage the "noise in my head" and make it coherent, yet I am taking in hundreds of colliding tones and voices and decisions through my ears. I remain unclear about the degree to which one can run in a serious way and listen at the same time, much less run and think, but I can form a proposition about this dual engagement and keep it moving. I am practicing a job involving concentration, and I am also opening myself to forces that will knock over the concentration, or reroute it, again and again.

Anyway: just as music can intensify the running, running can intensify the music. To intensify it means, for me, to make it vivid such that I can temporarily forget its after-the-fact form. Form in music is lovely and form is even sometimes necessary, I think, whether that means tonal resolution or tradition or narrative or salability or getting a job done. Form can complement what it contains. Freedom from form might be illusory, but at least let's go inside it so we can't see the edges.

o

Ten minutes into a run, I find my way: it happens while I notice the drummer of the Ohio Players. He plays rolls like nobody else—light, almost stumbling, fluttering lead-ups to an emphatic downbeat, never overdetermined. All right, then: he's going to be the key. I'll listen to him, I'll run alongside him. James "Diamond" Williams. I later find out that the record I'm listening to, *Pleasure*, was the first record he made with the group. Perhaps he wanted to be heard. He wanted to leave his signature in four or five places per song.

I don't want to admit it, but it's possible the music I choose to listen to as I run is limited by my preference for running in the morning, and there might be certain currents of thought I am reluctant to handle in the morning. The song "Pleasure" at first seems to be one of them: it's a riddle. Hard to do riddles in the morning.

This music is complicated—contrapuntal arrangements in the singing and the rhythm, so many vectors winging through it, live and all present all the time. The song is given more structure by the humor, or even more indirectly, the half steps into humor, the lines that venture toward ideas that outstrip its container. The Ohio Players contained a lot: one can imagine them hearing, from medium to long distance, many local musical traditions—in Dayton, Ohio, they were three hours from Detroit, five from Chicago, eight from Memphis, Tennessee, ten from New York, and twelve from New Orleans—and they were not imitating anything. They sound like themselves. They carried traces of P-Funk and Frank Zappa and Allen Toussaint and Sly Stone, and sometimes they were a beautifully anonymous jazz group with a Midwestern vernacular, and a jobbing R&B band, and a marching band, and sometimes they played ballads. None of them were solitary mountaintop virtuosos, but together on the flatlands they were brilliant.

Generally, I leave the house and think for a second about where I'd like to go and I go there. Often, along the way, I turn left or right at the last possible moment. One of my favorite words from earlier days of studying Latin is *praeceps*—usually an adjective, occasionally an adverb—which essentially means "headlong," or "headfirst." Often there is heedlessness or imminent danger implied in *praeceps*; the word "precipice" comes from it. But sometimes there is wisdom in it, as when Horace, describing the evolution of Roman theater in the *Ars Poetica*, described a new and fuller kind of flute-and-lyre playing, and a faster kind of stage speech, to accompany a more unrestrained and populist Roman theatergoing tradition: *facundia praeceps*. Headlong fluency.

When I run, as when I walk, the enterprise is entirely about moving forward; the difference with running is that momentum does half the moving for me. Reduced responsibility is added liberty. The running is "hard" at times, but my body adjusts to cope: long ago I settled into habits of landing on my forefoot, exhaling minimally, keeping my dorsal side up, and trying to lean back. Whatever hardness there is in running can be mitigated by the spirit I'm calling *praeceps*.

I might be running from something. I hope I am. I do feel a constant need to distance myself from some old assumption or reflex or sentimental attachment. Many of these arise in middle age, and they harden fast. Running at least gives me the freedom and optimism to imagine that such distancing may be possible. At most it gives me a lot more besides, so the necessity of *running from* may lead to the intention of *running to*. I would like to keep moving in the direction of intention, and figuring out what intention could be.

On the Ohio Players record I hear "Varee Is Love," an intention song, perhaps a desire song, really pretty—a woman named Varee, brass that is not in tune, it doesn't matter, it makes the song fuller. I have moved through the brachium-like trail leading out of the Parade Ground area and into the weird network of intersecting paths through the woods. Deep in the trees I hear "Funky Worm," still funny—the idea that the Moog synthesizer makes the sound of a worm, and the narration tells you about the worm, even though there isn't much to tell, and then essentially says, "There it is, look at it go!" and leaves you with a visual image as a keepsake. I'm running over dirt as I hear it, shifting among various different veins of trail, and imagining what's below my feet. During "Our Love Has Died" and its line "We buried our love six feet down," I am still thinking about the worms in the ground—the funky worm in the coffin. I hear Leroy Bonner shake a vowel like "ah-yah-yah-yah," as if he were snapping his wrist to dry a handful of parsley, and I think: "That's another thing Mick Jagger stole." I think of a college-radio DJ I heard one night in the '80s putting on an Ohio Players song after talking about how "adult" the fun in their music is. I'd never heard of that before, as a teenager—"adult fun."

It strikes me that in less than an hour of running with the Players, I have thought of the implications of counterpoint and the repeated signature, long-distance looking, love, death, appropriation, adulthood and maturity, "fun" (better with the quotation marks), the condition of moving-toward, and headlong fluency. It is possible that all these things are related to one another, and to running—or, better, that one could construct a graph for them that might look like a trail map of the park.

// 4 //

Allen Toussaint is gentle for a listener, and calm, a leader of calmness, so calm that as he sings he might not know how calm he is. In real life his manners were exquisite, radiant before he said a word. That really is a kind of power: how much a person can make clear about their relation to the world without using sound. Likewise, as a listener, you may assume from the first moments of one of his songs that Toussaint won't be shouting, and he won't be boosting his voice so high in the mix as to give himself an unfairly privileged relationship with the listener.

Instead, on the record *Toussaint*, he closely double-tracks his voice. That is both an industrial, finished-product idea—a reinforced barrier, cut twice to the same specifications, duplicated nearly precisely—and also a first-draft, sketch-mentality sort of idea, the practice of going over a line to shore it up, to make it thicker, and also to create a sense of discrepancy, a slight wriggliness to make it alive.

Now: sometimes he sings "mmm"—you can hear it in the chorus of "From a Whisper to a Scream." Check out the way he sings it. Not a basic body-pleasure "mmm," but specific and pointed, a straitened and economical version of happiness. I think he is making the floor of his mouth drop low. He might even be narrowing his cheeks, making the lower half of his face into a V shape. He brings out the trebly range of a bass-range sound. That's a kind of off-ness; you can relate it to the off-ness of swing rhythm. I imagine Toussaint making this face as he sings it, and I remember there are pictures of Thelonious Monk making this same face as he plays the piano. Allen Toussaint plays the piano, of course. So maybe it's a pianist's face.

As I listen to him in a working-class neighborhood in Yonkers, I run past the studio space of a great artist, one who practices a quietness around what he's doing relative to its enormousness. Toussaint and this artist can't be compared too closely. The artist rarely talks to interviewers; Toussaint made himself available. The artist wraps a layer of playful-sharp meta-commentary about art practice, audiences, boundaries, opportunity and inequity, and racism around his art. A similar awareness likely exists around Toussaint's art, because it would have to, but it may be so understated that some won't recognize it unless they look for it. I've run past the building many times before, because I like the building and I like thinking about the artist's persistence, but this time I see the inside of one part of it: the garage; I believe I see a ladder and a small forklift. The house, a one-story industrial property, is a wonder. It takes up half an outer-city block, and has reinforced windows. No words, no signage, no discernible mark of affluence, no evidence of people living there. It is what an undisclosed location looks like, with one exception: he recently put up a small sign on the side of the building that reads WASH YOUR, in rough red hand-painted letters, as on a lemonade stand, over two black-paint handprints.

The rough trail through the woods has dried up in the past few days—no spattering mud, but it's still hard to run on the old broken pavement and sharp stones where the trail has fallen apart. The trail suits horses. I have a feeling my feet are going to hurt later, and when I finally come out into the sun and the Van Cortlandt Parade Ground, they do. I'm all right with that.

o

Here is the runner I propose: enthusiastic but with no claim to expertise. If there is a way to run nearly every day without being an athlete, I'm going to find it. If goals define a runner, then I guess I am undefined. Running for me is light and air, and chaotic, kinetic intention: I don't know what this is, but this is what I am doing. Again, I don't count days off from running, measure or time myself, enter races (with few exceptions), keep a graded plan of increasing or decreasing miles, or save long runs for Sundays. If I did any of that, the chaos would be gone. The only days I miss are when I am sick; under the pressure of having to write, teach, or travel; or sufficiently happy or uninspired that running won't make a difference. Those days are useful, or at least they are part of a larger pattern of not wanting to repeat the same thing perfectly and only for its own sake. I agree with a version of the thought that Jenny Erpenbeck had her main character think in the novel *Go, Went, Gone*: "Anything predictable and rigid can be undermined and broken. Only chaos disrupts and remains."

o

About two-thirds of the way through Toussaint's record, and about two-thirds of the way through my desire to keep running, I come to "Working in the Coal Mine"—a good song for moving, because of its rhythmic wheels-within-wheels, and its singing horns, and Toussaint's reinforced gentleness, and the complex polyrhythmic logic of New Orleans four-beat, with so many little nodes and oil slicks in each measure. The background singers say, "Whoops!" on one of those slicks, just before the three. Toussaint retreats from the microphone for stretches of this record: he just plays his piano in the tidy machinery of the rhythm section, happy to be in the band. There are beats during these stretches when you can hear all the way around, 360 degrees. He winds the record up with "Pickles," and its rumbling Russian solo piano fantasias, after someone's harmonica solo. The wind pushes me along for the last twenty seconds of the song. I haven't listened to this record all the way through before, but I know this has to be the end of it, and I know this has to be the end of my run, so I stop and walk the rest of the way home.

A cold ending, but I'm grateful for it. There can't be many more of them. It's the first time I can remember being apprehensive about summer.

// 5 //

Often I want my running to feel like a Mal Waldron solo. I want it to be the weird, renewable, daily work of engrossed repetition.

If you look at music such that you are looking only for shapes with authority and definition, you will never see Mal Waldron, the pianist, born in 1925, died in 2002. I write "look at" and "see" (dammit), but I really mean something like "register in the ear as a special, autonomous event." I write "event" to keep things moving along, but the word is seldom accurate, and anyway, here I mean something closer to *icon*. The pre-digital meaning of the word "icon" is properly applied only to religious images, or—stretching it—to other images imbued by various beholders with quasi-religious meaning. An icon is a visual representation that stirs something inside, a grand symbol that forces a feeling of devotion, something that tends to provoke identification or ambition or possibly disgust. Why can't "icon" be used in the realm of sound? Let's stay within jazz alone—certain performances of operatic arias and the quick vocal runs called *taans* in Hindustani classical music would open up countless other possibilities. If we could use it, we'd call a lot of Charlie Parker's solos (and not only the famous ones) icons, as we would some of Max Roach's and Lester Young's and Sarah Vaughan's and Art Tatum's and Eric Dolphy's and Pharoah Sanders's and John Coltrane's, but Mal Waldron's we would not, because they weren't grand symbols.

Mal Waldron's solos observe harmony in motion and use syncopation but refuse to enter jazz's arena of competitive adornment. (He once made a Music Minus One record of Duke Ellington tunes, a functional service for developing musicians, in which he supplied the bare minimum such that soloists could play along to it, and though nobody suggests it as a record defining his singularity, it's *good*.) He comes up with an improvised phrase, never a very complicated one, and repeats it through a cycle of chords until the refusal to enlarge or modify it stretches credulity. To use "looking" terms again: it is as if he picks up something that is not exactly simple but is limited, of very finite and understandable parts—a baseball, let's say—and really, really looks at it. The act of looking is his solo.

He can seem to have hardly any guile, any fancy-dancing. It is as if he has taken his eye off the audience and become *engrossed*: as if at most he turns the baseball a quarter turn and then an eighth turn more and then back an eighth turn, measures with his finger joints the distance between where the seams come closest together and where they are farthest apart, scratches and picks at the seams with his fingernail, scuffs its surface against one kind of rock or another to test the resilience of the fiber, and never stops moving from one of these examinations to the next; they are all conjoined. But he doesn't seek to improve it or make something grander of it. He seldom uses a well-established musical move from the world outside his relationship to the phrase to make things cute; he doesn't use emotional clichés. He simply keeps working on his own rough and bumpy analysis, with no obvious payoff in sight, by which I mean in anticipated hearing.

He does this again and again until his playing becomes, without announcing itself as such, a philosophy of perseverance. He shows up and keeps at it. He was a good accompanist for singers and a good short-order tune-writer for hastily assembled recording sessions in the '50s and '60s, and after that he went forward, as money shrank in jazz and the times demanded new formats and venues: solos, duos, trios, quartets, art galleries, midsize theaters, European concert halls, whatever. He is one of the most recorded pianists in the jazz tradition, despite the fact that he wasn't technically impressive. He knew this, of course. "My technique was always nil and is still nil," he said to the radio interviewer Ted Panken. "I'm a rounded person. So whatever I hear, I know I can play, I know I can reach. In other words, if my technique isn't enough to cover it, then the idea doesn't come in my mind in the first place."

What did he say?

"A rounded person."

Say again?

A rounded person.

I don't know exactly what he meant by that, except possibly that he knew the dimensions of his rounded field. His perseverance and the strangeness of his repetitions and the realistic scale of his desire—not his virtuosity, because he didn't have any— suggested a future. Without having an exalted goal, he could keep doing the thing: that was enough.

After Allen Toussaint, I'm still thinking of New Orleans, and I am thinking of the New Orleans–ness of the drummer Ed Blackwell, who was born there in 1929. Today I listened to Eric Dolphy's record *At the Five Spot*, recorded live at that club in July 1961, with Mal Waldron on piano, Booker Little on trumpet, Richard Davis on bass, and Ed Blackwell on drums. The Five Spot, on Cooper Square in Manhattan's East Village, was a long, small room, a dozen tables and a bar, capacity around seventy-five. It barely needed amplification; in old pictures taken inside the club, only sometimes do you see horn players pointing their instruments toward microphones, but the musicians' sound had to travel all the way from the back to the front, where the club emptied out to the street. On this record, the tone of Blackwell's drums and cymbals cuts through the mix, and he seems to be imitating a dancer who keeps changing his moves, who never repeats an action quite the same way. I haven't listened to it closely in a few years. I've never thought about understanding the record better by running it.

I've turned off the cinder path around the Parade Ground and gone into the woods. Dolphy's soloing does rise to the level of the iconic through his poise, and his hard, bizarrely coiled phrases: He knows how he sounds. He knows he's different enough to be remembered. Listen to the way he gets so close to the heat of his ideation: What is he thinking about? His phrases don't move like people. They settle briefly and then scatter. He is likely to be thinking about animals. He is likely to be thinking about birds—whereas Booker Little's trumpet soloing is clean, delimited, declarative, intellectually strong; it holds dissonances and microtonal pitches and keeps them aglow. Booker Little, you suspect, is the one who's really going to make it in this world, but he died three months later of uremia.

I'm running through a city-country trail deep in the park, with rocks and roots and old, pitted pavement. And now here comes Mal Waldron, feeling every rock in the trail: "Yes, I'm here; that's interesting; that's interesting too; what happens if you turn that over; I'm going to move these stones over to the left; time to make an adjustment; the ground is wet here;

I see some planks over a streambed; perhaps I'll get my shoes slightly wet; the swamp-rot smell is pleasing; I am continuing to go forward." He is doing this; I am doing this. Together we build proprioception—an awareness of the body relative to its spatial surroundings. I hear myself think, "This is the same solo he played on the last track!" But a few paces later I realize it's not really. Pointed toward icons, I am looking for the authority of distinction—the memory of the shape set against the clear sky. He's doing something else, something brushy, fuzzy, without clean beginnings or ends.

This is a time to be thinking about the long game, and to look back at those who practiced the long game well. Mal Waldron's is about the best I can imagine. He came to his feet during a fraught stage of the American long game, particularly from 1961 to 1963, when we were more or less forced to face unfaceable acts of division or exclosure at home and abroad—the beating of Freedom Riders, the standoff with Cuba, the building of the Berlin Wall—and to realize the limitations of our distinctness and specialness and neatness, and form a new sensibility. Individual acts of heroism were not the only meaningful response. A certain gray ambivalence and a wary kind of waiting seemed not an absence but a presence.

o

Yvonne Rainer's movement-performance piece *We Shall Run* came along a few years after Dolphy's Five Spot recording, in 1963. It was created for a performance in a gymnasium space within the Judson Memorial Church on Washington Square South in New York City. Twelve dancers line up with their backs to a long wall; they begin jogging to a recording of the *tuba mirum* section of Hector Berlioz's *Requiem,* and continue for seven minutes. The dancers first run in the same direction as one another, and then groups of varying sizes quickly veer in varying directions; Rainer's sequence of directions is quite explicit. After this complicated splintering, the dancers end up running in a giant circle toward the middle of the floor. But everyone evenly persists and nobody does anything heroic, and because anybody—dancers and nondancers—can perform this piece, anybody watching it can feel implicated. There is no significant link between the plotted movements and the music, perhaps other than the fact that both involve a group of people working in groups on a coordinated task; the *Requiem* is scored for an orchestra as well as 210 singers, split between sopranos, altos, tenors, and basses. The seeming disparity between the music and the movement might be part of the point. Rainer was proving you can run to any music.

I listen to more of the Eric Dolphy record. Booker Little, at some point, starts playing the melody of "How High the Moon" for three seconds to propel himself forward into the next chapter of his improvisation. He will accept a ready-made; he will put the quotation marks on. Waldron won't. Somewhere else on the record, you can hear Waldron start to form an idea with a vague relation to the first four notes of Thelonious Monk's "Pannonica," but he does not want you to recognize it and he is not going to continue it—instinctively, he backs up and plays that shard, those four notes, again and again until they are unfamiliar.

Now that I am warmed up and heading back out toward the Parade Ground, I am invigorated, but more than that, I am persevering. I'm in Waldron's spell—I will continue moving for the sake of moving—the point of it will come clear later, by accumulation, if it ever needs to. We shall run. I decide not to run around the flat periphery trails but right through the rise in the middle of the park, Vault Hill. This is near the fenced burial ground of the Van Cortlandts, the Dutch mercantile family who had farms and a mansion on the property. They bought the land in 1694 from Adriaen van der Donck, who had in turn bought it from the Dutch East India Company in 1646. The Wiechquaskeck Lenape Indians, who had settled and lived on the land for more than six hundred years before the arrival of the Dutch, seem to have buried their dead on the land that now comprises the southwestern quadrant of the Parade Ground. The people enslaved by Jacobus van Cortlandt were buried in an area—unmarked, like the Lenapes—to the east of the family mansion, by the pond they had created to power a mill. I often think about how a fence casts a warning against running on any kind of verified living, but also any kind of verified deadness. I can't run on the Dutch dead: they are fenced in. I have no idea how many Lenape or African dead I run on every day.

The route through the middle of the rise and over the hill, as opposed to on the flatter area around it, makes the running "hard," because the rise is steep; it also honors Mal Waldron's fierce loyalty to the area around middle C. But the running is really not so hard. Daily practice of any kind is rough and rocky and leafy and full of roots and bumps and breaks. This is the "same" thing I did two days ago, on a path I have run hundreds of times, and just as it is not ever hard, it is not ever the same.

"The Prophet" on this record, twenty-one minutes long, is so astonishing that I listen a second time. This *praeceps*-leaping and thoroughgoing investigation, this collective dancing and theorizing, all Dolphy's voluble action from the front of the brain and the middle of the heart, the handsome structure of it—fifty-six concise notes across a thirty-two-bar theme; then choruses and choruses of solos by everyone, starting with Dolphy, as provocative and diffuse and restive as he can get; the ensemble theme again, and then, as if to proclaim, "Don't forget who wrote this," one last solo chorus from Dolphy, in which he keeps it thrillingly legit, close to orthodoxy, close to Charlie Parker—were performed for fewer than one hundred people. How could that be? I consider that I am running and listening, and the air is clean, and the sun is out, and it is late spring, and I am "working," doing something that seems "hard," and I don't know what it is, but it is what I'm doing, and I'm doing it for nobody.

// 6 //

I remember the first time I saw a runner with a movement I coveted, years ago: long stride, long limbs, steady waist, flexible hips, even more flexible shoulder line, as if they were converting the hardness of the road into bounce—a lot of expending and then gathering. It's strange but sweet that I don't remember what gender I thought the runner was. In my memory this person was virtuosic—the only comparison I reach for is to Marie Bryant, the luminous dancer in Gjon Mili's short film *Jammin' the Blues*. Bryant was known for a method of movement she called "controlled release"—she once described it as "finding the natural line in each body and the favorite ways it likes to move about—then controlling these movements." Joy first, discipline second.

But I see more often in comfortable, experienced runners a light and upright motion of small steps, torso erect, shoulders back, forearms a little less than ninety degrees from the upper arms, fists closed gently as if holding reins. It looks clipped and sustainable, Blackwellian, with a smaller area around the beat. It is a kind of running that seems to have no awareness of breath or clock time: it is a way of holding energy in a fixed position.

Ed Blackwell's drumming rhythm never begins with some mid-century idea of "jazz"—it suggests something bigger, like the idea of public-sphere dancing—dancing at events that are outdoor, free, cross-generational, without an advertising agenda; functions that started before you were born. He could look at a drum—or, better yet, two, but sometimes not more than two—and get to work without the need for teasing, elegant approaches. Like Waldron, he can seem almost guileless, especially when his patterns between two drums are one hit on drum A, one hit on drum B, one hit on drum A, one hit on drum B . . . he *just begins*, and continues with strength and precision. Such a description ignores what he does with cymbals, so casual and powerful— there but almost not there, his hi-hat swing on the two and four, his unforced maintenance on the ride cymbal, as if he were watering it, maybe while looking the other way. This is how to be original and unpretentious at the same time.

I want to listen to more Blackwell because he sets pretty good runner tempos, if I want or believe in such things—variations of high-medium—and holds them steady enough to hook you entirely. But tempos aren't everything. Runners can also respond to a musician's engagement and aliveness—the condition of being *on*—on for themselves, as opposed to for us. Blackwell's beat keeps its back straight, like a drum-corps player, and bounces lightly. I keep my back straight in sympathy. Its strength lies in the middle: light bass drum, light cymbals. It is not overbearing. It turns on and turns off and doesn't wear itself out. It can make you a better runner, the kind who runs first for the feeling, and second the discipline: controlled release. Ideally, I want to move like Ed Blackwell plays.

I want to hear Blackwell with less going on around him than the four other musicians in Eric Dolphy's band, so I think of his duo records from the early '80s: *El Corazón*, with the trumpeter Don Cherry; and *Red and Black in Willisau*, with the tenor saxophonist Dewey Redman, from a time when there was so little money in improvised music that the low-cost format of free-improvising duets almost became its own genre. But the best duos, between people who know each other well, don't suggest scarcity: in these cases there can seem to be more knowledge and information flying between two people than among four or five. The information can arrive in silences, in sudden turnbacks and refusals; or in acquiescences, covenants of spooky energy and allowance.

Don Cherry, on *El Corazón*, is serene or choppy, aiming over or right at Blackwell. Dewey Redman, on *Red and Black in Willisau*—as if in another time and place, on tenor saxophone—plays longer swing phrases, or sometimes minimal two- and three-note patterns accompanied by his own vocal tones and screams—through his nose? Around the mouthpiece? They come out however they can.

This is music divided into sections by ongoing instinct, given names later, and it doesn't really need the medium of the album. It doesn't have much of a plan—it lives entirely in the present. Every step of the way it proceeds in line with how I like to think about running.

Today has brought the first true sign of summer—the temperature probably rises ten degrees during the hour I am outside. Blackwell assures us that the music is so rhythmic that it will not let you flag. Up at 261st Street I have to take off my jacket, sometimes a pitiful thing to have to do when you are in motion, but I love having a reason to stop and move in place, reacting to Blackwell's rhythms with a version of boxing footwork.

I am conditioned to keep searching for music I don't know, and I don't think I will ever stop, but I can imagine ending the search here and simply deciding, "This is the music for me"—not just for running, but for living. This thought comes at the top of a precipitous downhill road parallel to the Hudson River. I've gotten to the top and I've got a long, clear shot toward the bottom. Perhaps this is the reason I'm considering what it means to set a course for life.

This music, these dialogues between drums and one other instrument, are what describes my intent; this seems to be my desired point of view. Why this music? Because it has no lyrics and no story; because it is inviting, disinterested in commerce but open to almost anything, ready to play, recognizable to adults and children; because it has no airs. It doesn't need to win. It sounds like the music of today and of two hundred years ago. These three musicians shared these musical values. There's not a lot of this kind of thing in the world; is there enough of it to last the rest of my life? Sure there is. If I love it sufficiently, there is enough. To love anything is to be satisfied by what's already there.

But to think about "the rest of my life" would mean becoming oriented around an end point, a place to stop, the end of a life. I am determined not to stop. So if I have to forget about Ed Blackwell tomorrow, that's what I'll do. The choice right now is between moving forward and . . . I can't remember what the other option is.

// 7 //

Down at the Van Cortlandt Stadium, I see a woman around my age running sprint laps around the track. She is tall and solid and self-possessed, and has a running shape Alan Lomax might have called "solid trunk and linear movement," when he made his strange documentary *Dance and Human History*—a film proposing a catalog of body-movement patterns around the knowledge system he called choreometrics. The sprinter registers her laps with style; she wears sneakers of two different colors, one red and one green. I have a strong passing thought that I'd like to be her. What power, to have that control and strength, to run that fast in measured amounts, as you like. What power. Between sprints she walks on the field inside the track, with her hands on her hips, looking at everything and nothing.

When one runs, it is possible to feel within oneself to an extreme: as you are in motion, raising your heart rate, you rediscover the unity of your own body and its particulars—your own head, neck, shoulders, elbows, forearms, hips, thighs, calves, feet. If you run while listening to music, it is also possible to get *outside* of yourself and imagine yourself in collaboration with another, if only the musician whom you are listening to. This may be what various kinds of scholars call intersubjectivity, though I'm not sure I should be using the word lightly or at all. Anyway, I am describing the feeling of being both profoundly within yourself and profoundly near another.

In both conditions there are responsibilities. Within yourself you must practice balance, take care not to fall over, make sure you don't knock into anyone else or scrape, break, or burn your own body. As adjunct or all-but-conjunct to another, you must take heed: What might it be like to be that person? What impels them? What are their responsibilities? What is that person moving toward?

It seems to me that the desire to be somebody else is not a symptom of self-annihilation but of strength. You can't *be* the other person—that is the problem, but it's also the upside. It will never happen. If copying that person exactly seems like the next best thing, the desire is only a delusion. The congruence will never be complete. But you can have a moment of blind desire, when you simply want unaccountable transference of energy from someone else—when you have the following thought: "I can learn much from you but I don't know what, and perhaps my life will change in some small way." I'm calling this thought desire, but it deserves a subcategory. I don't want to think of it as a belief; I'll call it a study.

I remember that desire from childhood, and it passed out of my repertoire. As an adult one can feel some pressure to get rid of old study-desires to be another, or to keep a distance from them. Better to desire to be yourself: much of your life depends on learning to do that. You repeat to yourself the question asked by Bonbon, the protagonist of Paul Beatty's novel *The Sellout*: "Who am I? and How may I become myself?" If you let go of either part of that question, you may be in trouble.

My thoughts during running are mostly in the spirit of the

advancing now, not of retrospection. And if I listen to music that suggests the most hurtling-forward motion, I can that much more easily understand the logic of the music, and think my own thoughts through that logic and *become* the music. I am listening to the Chicago hardcore band C.H.E.W., everything it did, particularly the record *Feeding Frenzy* and its split EP, *Strange New Universe*, with Penetrode, also from Chicago. C.H.E.W. uses the D-beat, the beat of the early-'80s English punk band Discharge—a skipping beat, like the Antillean *tresillo*. It's like an old folk or rock-and-roll two-beat rhythm—like the beat of polka or a lot of traditional Mexican dance music—but twice as fast, and with a skip or a stutter to add swing before the fourth beat.

The singer of C.H.E.W., Doris Jeane, is a kind of sprinter. Her singing, or screaming, on "Futile Pursuit" and "Negative Nancy," becomes flung matter, hard and intense; she is the projectile—the matter is Doris herself. She varies her strategy: rapid syllables, long and floating groans and screams, hard shakes of the microphone to make a juddering tremolo sound. She generates catharsis this way, and it seems to me the catharsis grows more real when the subject of the song remains unclear, or just beyond outside comprehension—when the best a listener can do is decide that the motion *is* the idea. Intensely alive, she feels for small openings, places to bounce and pivot, ways to continue skipping and swinging through it, at speed! A song ends and demands that another one follow it immediately.

I suppose it's no accident that the ethos of hardcore tends toward communal living, nonhierarchical living, and records that aren't particularly distinct, that aren't isolated masterpieces or institutions. Likewise, the best hardcore bands, like C.H.E.W., often suddenly disappear: maybe their members had a disagreement that made working together more trouble than it was worth, or someone moved or started a job and no longer had time for touring. Easy come, easy go. They try to find a common cause and to make short, modular blasts of slate-gray sound in a sequence that could conceivably go on forever; they don't sculpt them together into a story or a perfect shape. Perhaps they don't want to get to know the music too well, or so well that it becomes a closed system with a fixed value, something that becomes trapped, or that could trap them. They leave it up to you, another participant in their endeavor, to move through it and create value in it.

o

In her autobiography, *Feelings Are Facts*, Yvonne Rainer reports that in July 1959, she wrote the following in a letter to her brother, by way of explaining what "dance" meant to her:

Dance=
1. A way out of an emotional dilemma.
2. A place where the training period is so long and arduous as to almost indefinitely postpone a coming to grips with things like purpose and aesthetic or vocational direction.
3. A place that offers some rarer moments of "rightness" (that word again; I think it is equivalent to joy, or "fitness," i.e., things fit).
4. Something that makes my throat fill up sometimes.
5. Something to do every day.
6. A way of life, where most other things in a life assume a lesser importance and value.

7. Something that offers an identity: "I am a dancer," also "I am a hard worker, I work my ass off in class in spite of being handicapped by a crazy Rainer body." The virtue of hard work, salvation through sweat, is very important here. I am sure most dancers are martyrs of one variety or another.

I feel some connection to selected parts of this list and to Rainer. She performed her dance projects at the Judson Memorial Church in New York City in the early 1960s soon after my father moved out of a building adjoining that church—they walked the same ground. As a younger person (and in a more tempered way as an older person), she was fascinated by some of the subjects I have been thinking about a lot: cliché, virtuosity, the problems of narrative. And she put running into her choreography very early—*We Shall Run* is dance as organized running.

Her list also includes much struggle and self-criticism. Naturally, any artistic movement as powerful as the one Rainer incited ought to be understood as brave and risky, a reaction to something external—a state of affairs she isn't willing to put up with. As for me, I haven't had a "training period" as a runner, I'm not running for an audience, and I do not run with the knowledge that I am corresponding with or disputing any ongoing tradition of running. (For instance, I don't think anyone needs to argue for running while listening to music, since so many people already do it. I only want to consider what running and listening have to do with each other.) I'm not particularly reacting against anything external—in fact, I could start running only once I had established a fair amount of peace in my life.

As for training, I don't want to let running gain the upper

hand over me. Running has organized my life and tenderized me with unexpected force—if I trained, I can imagine getting too involved in it. Family tradition, as well as the professional molding of criticism and its imprecise but useful myth of "critical distance," and, I guess, personal inclination, has led me to this wariness. In music I have spent a lot of time around brilliant people who have great enthusiasms and insecurities. To write about them, I must leave their parties early. Likewise, I am not part of a community of runners. I take this position because I like to be alone among others. I don't want to be in a club with runners, because I would be beholden to them, and I don't want to be in a club with running, because I would be beholden to it.

I find that a good way of keeping my distance from running, while looking forward to it, is to listen to music while I run. This way I am not in it only for the running.

// 8 //

From two musicians—Ed Blackwell and Don Cherry—down to one. I don't know much of the music very well on this record, the pianist Víkingur Ólafsson's *Debussy-Rameau*—but a friend recommended it, and his word is good enough for me.

I like the exercise of pairing an A and a B who seem separated by reasons of time period or geography or school of thought. Put them together and see what happens. But don't arrange them into a story that's destined to become an opinion, or that's aimed at a fixed point of view. (Francis Bacon, talking to David Sylvester in 1961, the year of Dolphy's *At the Five Spot*: "The moment there are several figures—at any rate several figures on the same canvas—the story begins to be elaborated. And the moment the story is elaborated, the boredom sets in; the story talks louder than the paint.") Trust them to push the exercise forward, so that the pairing retains the power to sharpen one's perception. I still think about a solo viola concert Kim Kashkashian gave, alternating between Bach and the contemporary composer György Kurtág: that was a thrilling hour in my life. And so we have Debussy and Rameau, writing solo piano music something like 175 years apart. I don't know their shared history, other than that they were both French, and as I run, I barely think about where Debussy ends and Rameau begins.

O

A few years ago, when I was having trouble turning a small idea into a big idea, I started to go on longer and longer runs. The urge was to make a metaphorical idea come true: by tracing a bigger area with my feet, perhaps I could trace a bigger area with my mind.

I am doing something like that now, running to alter my thinking, but this time the running isn't about tracing a large area as much as going into a place unknown to me. After a while, the only thing that many writers wish for is the ability to change their own perception. This takes more than input or learning. You can talk to hundreds of people, read hundreds of books, do a lot of preparation, and still be stuck with more or less the same perception, the same limited set of ideas. This sort of perceptual change is an abstract wish and an abstract achievement—it's all in the brain. By changing my perception physically, I thought I might help the process.

John Berger wrote a short essay called "Field." He was a little younger than I am now, having written art criticism for twenty years, and having come to doubt its protocols, to resent both the professional practice of "criticism" and the social construction of "art," and essentially setting himself up for a kind of intellectual suicide or rebirth. "Field" was published in *New Society* in November 1971, a few months before his television series *Ways of Seeing* and the published-book version of the series, both of which would change his life. It reads like a tense dramatic monologue. It may not be clear at first what the essay is about, and that is because it is not about a thing or a stable idea but the real-time sensation of expanding one's perception.

It is written from the vantage point of the driver's seat in Berger's car. He has stopped at a railroad crossing outside of Geneva to wait for a train to pass. Where is this railroad crossing? He does not say, but if you look up some facts about his life, and learn that he lived then in the Swiss town of Meyrin, he essentially tells you how to get there.

"From the city centre," he writes, "there are two ways back to the satellite city in which I live: the main road with a lot of traffic, and a side road which goes over a level crossing." As he describes the spot, it could have been one of the open green places at the intersection of the Route de Meyrin and the Route du Mandement, where Google Street View now shows a traffic circle and a level crossing. If this is true, I find by zooming out a bit, Berger's field is located about a third of a mile, or a ten-minute walk, from where the internet would be developed nineteen years later by the British computer scientist Tim Berners-Lee, in one of the buildings of CERN, the physics-research laboratory. Because "Field" is such a dimension-connecting and thus internet-like piece of writing, and because I had to use the internet to find a picture of the field, I find the location of the field a little uncanny.

Berger is looking out the window at a field abutting the railroad. This field, he explains, exists for him only as something pleasant to drive past on the way to his apartment, yet he wonders why he never looks at it more, and why he never bothers to walk to it from home. Within his daily experience, it is a container of nature or animals, but not much of an entity in itself. He finds the situation all wrong and wonders how to correct it. So he begins with an act of creative squinting: I know what this thing is, but forget about what I know: What is it *like*, and what does it suggest?

"Shelf of a field, green, within easy reach, the grass on it not yet high, papered with blue sky through which yellow has grown to make pure green." The field is "friable at its edges, the corners of it rounded": this is the voice of a person scrunching his eyes, making a conscious effort to see something in a new way and to describe it using language less facile than whatever comes to mind first. The field becomes the addressee, and the addressee becomes something other than a field. What is it? He's not sure. He's persevering.

In the next paragraph, Berger thinks about music.

> Remember what it was like to be sung to sleep. If you are fortunate, the memory will be more recent than childhood. The repeated lines of words and music are like paths. These paths are circular and the rings they make are linked together like those of a chain. You walk along these paths and are led by them in circles which lead from one to the other, further and further away. The field upon which you walk and upon which the chain is laid is the song.

Perhaps he himself is filling time by singing a song as he waits, and the field fills his eyes as the song fills the minutes, and the minutes fill . . . "It is as though these minutes fill a certain area of time which exactly fits the spatial area of the field," he writes. "Time and space conjoin." The sound of a hen in a garden near the field—not an occurrence in the field, but something off to the side that he can't see—strikes him as an "event." He chooses to pay attention to that event, and this brings him to "an intense awareness of freedom."

End of the third paragraph: "I knew that in that field I could listen to all sounds, all music."

What did he say?

"I knew that in that field I could listen to all sounds, all music."

Say again?

I knew that in that field I could listen to all sounds, all music.

Every day I take inventory of my own field—it is not just the Van Cortlandt field, but also my larger field of marsh and woodlands and street—following a song that I know distantly but not too well. I also know I can listen to anything in this field, and that the field is the song because the song becomes the field, or makes the field real to me. I know that I am listening to the field as I am listening to the song. Which really means I am listening to my own movement around or amid the field. In this way, the running is the song.

John Berger wrote a lot about art and images but almost nothing about music. Perhaps he felt music was outside his area of expertise, or that he wasn't a particularly skilled listener, or that music didn't need his help. Perhaps he read just enough of music's historical and critical literature to know he didn't trust it. But the scant references he made to music suggest he understood music in terms of time, distance, absence, and a proposed future. Music "offers time a center," as he put it in 1985, in the television video essay *About Time*. Thirty years later, he wrote: "Songs are sung to an absence. Absence is what inspired them, and it's what they address."

To take up the invitation of "Field": one assumes the dimensions of one's daily experience. The negative way of realizing this may be through reducing lived life to the procedure of getting rid of it: pissing your life away, crossing another day off the list. Another, more positive way of realizing it might be through elevating lived life to the interesting fact of being ongoing in it.

○

As I hear Rameau and Debussy spliced together in a way I can register but not quite contain, by instinct I feel some sort of similar desire to splice. I push into a part of the park I don't know, between Interstate 87 and the Mosholu Parkway, up to the Old Croton Aqueduct Trail: a narrow and simple passageway through the woods, between a high slope (east into the Bronx) and a low dip (the lowlands of Broadway, and beyond it the valley north of the Harlem River).

Ólafsson chimes on, making his trails distinct and useful: he clears the brush and doesn't leave much of his own ego behind. It seems I can perceive the paths differently via the movement of the music, chords of green and brown and blue, a range of high and low elevations, not only the unlikely stretch of woods in an urban pocket between highways, but the unlikely path from Debussy to Rameau. (Ólafsson calls the record an "impossible conversation.") The instability in the "Préludes" and "Images," whose tonal worlds give us the sense that we don't know where we are or where we're going, becomes complementary to Rameau's ravenous narrative logic.

As I head south on the trail, a man approaches me very slowly on a bicycle with his mask down just enough that I can see his face. Short, White, Irish looking, early thirties. He really studies me hard, analyzing me in the brief encounter, not so much with hostility but with high hopes. I'm not sure what that means. Shortly after, I run past a small boy astride a bicycle, standing still, his feet on the ground, also with his mask somewhat down. He has a similar face and offers a similar expression. A couple of seconds later he yells ahead: *"Can I go?"*

I don't know, can you? Sometimes there are people sleeping rough near the trail. It has a generally abandoned feeling. People are wary of all kinds of things now. I'm not sure what this exchange is about, but I have one idea: the man saw a big moving body at a distance, maybe looking a little unusual, with one bandanna on his head and another over his face—me—and took the lead in order to make sure I wasn't going to pose any danger.

The man might have been worried for his own safety, or for the safety of the boy. (I have a friend who gave up running in this park because she didn't feel safe.) There is equal opportunity for danger and freedom in solo running and in solo music. If you are the performer, a solo performance rests on you: the line, the balance, the narrative or lack of narrative. There is a lot to carry, which is a danger, but the responsibility may be offset by the lack of proprioceptive risk, which may be freedom. What you feel is never wrong in relation to anyone else, because there is nobody else to bang into.

Let's say I've gone running four thousand times. I've probably run with other people only about fifty times. I don't seek out strangers to run with; if there are pickup running groups in my area, I haven't heard of them. It is rare for me to encounter a stranger who approaches and runs-and-talks alongside me; it's happened to me only once. The ethos of running involves letting other people have their space and dignity. Sometimes it's as if we're all solo performers playing Debussy on our routes, and we afford one another professional respect as we pass. You're not going to sit down next to Ólafsson, or any pianist, during their performance and start playing your own thing. Nobody does that. (Bud Powell used to do it in jazz clubs, but his mental balance wasn't so good.) I have trained myself as a soloist without ever thinking about it— soloing is what I am doing. Soloists aren't simply playing with others, minus the others: the solo performance is a distinct category of performance. But soloists probably do what they do in order to better understand their place in relation to others, and to the world.

// 9 //

"All sounds, all music." I wonder what it might be like to run with the stillest, quietest, calmest music I can think of, music that has nothing to do with regular rhythm or the quality of an "event." Takahashi Kuzan, born in 1900, recorded an album called *Take no Hibiki*, self-released, date unknown, though possibly he made it toward the end of his life, in the 1980s. *Take no Hibiki* can translate either to "the sound of bamboo" or "the echo of bamboo." An implication of the present and the past at once.

Kuzan played the shakuhachi, a bamboo instrument with four holes, held like a recorder. Typically he plays one extended phrase; then he breathes in, for a kind of unheard phrase of silence; then he plays the next phrase. Rarely do his notes go above whisper volume, but they all retain a sort of power, a seriousness. He paces himself on those exhalations, and the instrument lets you hear all the frailty and trembling in his breath, even if he is not always breathing out to the end of his lung capacity.

Kuzan worked with a predetermined style and repertory, but above all an intent that traces back to the seventeenth century, to the roaming monks of the Fuke sect, who played the instrument for alms, then during the meditation sessions of others. Their practice was called *suizen*, or "blowing Zen," and they were called *komuso*, "monks of emptiness." In public, they were known for wearing woven baskets on their heads and concealing their faces as they played, to imply an erased self. Kuzan, presumably, didn't do this; he was secular: a musician, not a monk.

Within a minute of listening to the record you feel you are hearing a life's work basically compressed within each phrase, and expressed through a medium of very limited output. Kuzan's project was about meditation—yes, it was—but also the transmission of a set of centuries-old musical works, which he knew and taught, called *honkyoku*. Since the meditation practice came from routing air through the instrument, the music is about breath, but it is also about the spaces between breaths. Kuzan looks quite old in the picture on the record cover, and of course his lungs might have been better than mine, but you do seem to hear a finality in each phrase, as if he were saying, "This is what I am, and it's all I am," or as if he were expiring after each one.

Kuzan's record begins with a version of "Kyorei," or "Empty Bell," one of the oldest known pieces of the *honkyoku*. The phrases are sparse. One note; two notes; one note; two notes; four notes; five notes. In this music, one assumes, the excellence of a player seems to be measured by a quality of purpose, a spirit equal to the music's form, with a self that recedes before it. If it's about narrative, I can't hear it. The long tones are impressive, but they barely register as feats, much less as one of Berger's "events." I can't sense an "arc," and I certainly don't know when each piece is going to end; the phrasing never forecasts it.

o

Another shakuhachi player, Hisamatsu Fuyo, who died in 1871, asked himself in a written self-interview—as a document, one

of the most remarkable artist's statements I've ever seen—
what makes a good shakuhachi player, and what makes a master? Here was his response:

> A master naturally and effortlessly brings forth something
> inconceivable. However, without study it is impossible to
> enter the boundaries of mastery. You become the bamboo.
> The bamboo becomes you. A master lives in emptiness while
> working in form. Then playing each piece becomes Kyorei.
> Emptiness is taking the name of Kyorei as the essence of
> each piece.

You can listen into another's breathing and lose track of your own, just as you can assume another's stride. Kuzan's breathing is careful and imposing, even while it is barely there. To the extent that he's become the bamboo, his playing reminds me of the day, a month or so after I began running, when I realized I hadn't thought about my breathing once—when a runner's breathing, which can seem to be everything, became nothing. Most impressively, Kuzan is not playing in regular time. For a while I try to count the beats, like a running conductor, but it won't work. His phrasing never adheres to consistent pulse.

Strange how energizing this very still music can be. I find myself charging up hills, changing my route several times at the last second in order to encounter more of them, perhaps to feel my own breathing more acutely, or to locate the point at which a great awareness of breathing can be matched by a great forgetting. In some of the pieces on *Take no Hibiki*, Kuzan double-tracks his shakuhachi, playing unison lines with himself, which seems to me an amazing feat; he has internalized a procession of personal phrases that aren't dependent on a regular rhythm. Since I'm running on the usual messed-up trails, full of rocks and divots, the roughness of his tone and delivery pleases me: the bamboo produces tiny rasps, including one in the first microsecond of "Kyorei," like a tiny bit of feedback before a guitarist's opening chord. I make a few sloppy ascents on these hills, in very irregular rhythms myself, but while entraining with these long tones, I don't particularly care.

// 10 //

For a long time I didn't listen to Alice Coltrane much, because I felt her music wasn't telling me anything in particular or asking me anything that I was prepared to answer. I heard it as coming with a set of signifiers—modal jazz from the '60s, and then, later, something more specific and recondite: music for meditation and prayer within the Vedantic tradition. Most music comes with signifiers, but I experienced the ones around her music as loud, perhaps louder than the music itself. As most music has signifiers, most music also has a brief, a function. I suppose I didn't quite see myself as part of the brief of Alice Coltrane's music, or really appreciate what its brief was.

To the great extent that she made music for the purpose of partaking in a spiritual endeavor, a particular spiritual understanding of the world for spiritual people, I felt apart from it. And anyone who loves Alice Coltrane's music because it seems to gather a listener in, because it may offer an ethos of understanding, might be puzzled at my other general feeling, about the sound itself: I felt that it pushed me out. It contains so much of her arpeggiated motion on the keyboard and harp, so many rolling chords and modes, up and down, up and down, not in short phrases, and not particularly gestural or pointed. It can seem urgent and also impassive, and somehow, for me, this pairing didn't result in any kind of neat paradox, perhaps because I couldn't see the end of it, by which I mean I couldn't hear the end of it. It suggested such an endless supply of waves and troughs, peaks and swales, never staying up or down for very long—that I couldn't find the opening in it as a listener. I imagined myself on the outside, wondering what to do.

I remember having drinks with a writer friend once. She asked me what I thought about Alice Coltrane, and I told her, and her memorably intense response was this: "So is Alice Coltrane just a *convenient lacuna* for you?"

That was very well put. She was smiling but not laughing. I laugh as I write this, and "convenient" still stings, but she was only being precise. At the root I felt that John was my subject, my deep interest, Alice less so, and if I'm telling myself I'm more interested in music than in musicians' lives, then of course I can like what I like, but I am less sure now what that distinction means, and even so, I was using the logic of needing to not think about A in order to think about B. And this is an old story, since A was B's wife and B was A's husband.

Running has clarified things. Because the direction of Alice Coltrane's music doesn't change course decisively, I feel as I run that I am not simply reacting to its positions, I am moving with them. If I still sometimes find the music dense, if I can't get into the spaces of it, I can run alongside it.

Huntington Ashram Monastery suits the limited means of running: only three musicians, recorded in the basement of her home, dry and resonant and to the point. (From a musician who thought in great quantities of sound, it feels helpfully delimited.) All her music carries a drift not of commerce or entertainment but of daily practice. There are two aspects of it here, in particular, that correspond with my own. One is how she starts playing and one is how she stops playing.

When I begin to run, I try not to think about it, or, better to say, I don't think about it; I just begin, such that a minute later I might notice I am running and think, "Oh, so I've begun." Intention is wonderful, but I would like only the intention to fall into running, as if a breath of wind had tipped me off a ledge. Too much consideration of the switch from walking to running strikes me as self-important, anyway. Where am I going so quickly?

Similarly, Alice Coltrane seldom begins with a theme, a melody, or a flourish; she never begins with a gesture of "and now I will play you a song." She might begin by vamping, playing repeated riffs, which you feel certain will keep thickening and repeating, or turn into her usual cloudlike shapes; or she might begin by implying a set of chords that she connects with so much arpeggiated floss, the paralanguage of a tune, that you can't really tell what's the tune and what's the daily practice. Really: her version of "Turiya" on *Huntington Ashram Monastery*, with Coltrane playing the harp alongside the bassist Ron Carter and drummer Rashied Ali, is wall-to-wall Alice. For more than four minutes, you never stop hearing her. This is the way to begin running. Not a "work"; a practice. Not an event per se: we shall begin and then go on.

Her beginnings are the music of looking around, blinking in the light, breathing, stretching your neck. And then there is the way she ends before another musician's turn to solo: I noticed it best on "Via Sivanandagar."

She has been improvising steadily for three minutes straight over the rhythm section, playing at a rapid tempo, building up her clouds, making wise, judicious fourth chords with her left hand, letting them ring in the air, and then she comes to a graceful end—not at the end of a four-bar phrase or some other recognizable unit of music, but simply when she has said enough. She has been playing at the extreme ends of the piano; the low notes resound for a few seconds; then she takes her foot off the pedal and she stops running. The other musicians take over and begin to improvise. She doesn't act like a piano-trio bandleader when they solo, prodding them or feeding them comping chords. She just lets them carry on for a minute and then reenters as if moved by gravity.

I know it's recorded in a studio; I know that the studio is in her house. I wouldn't be too surprised if no one else were in the room, or even in an outside booth. The room casts a neutral tone. There is a profound sense here of music not being made for an audience.

I find the beginning of the piece alluring, but when I hear her withdrawal—as quick, private, and non-grandiose an action as closing one's eyes—I can hear what I haven't yet heard: the way to get into her music, and to run alongside it, in its spirit. I don't have a desire to stop, so as to be in agreement with her; I don't mean that. I want to continue moving in the space she's cleared. Her sound, continuous, rumbles on in the mind after she's stopped, but her playing exerts an influence to keep moving in its absence.

// 11 //

A few words about earphones. Since 1980 or so, when the Sony Walkman entered the commercial market outside Japan, great numbers of people adapted very quickly to the idea of moving physically while music played via a dedicated feed to one's own ears and nobody else's. In America, at least, the rise of the Walkman moved into the back draft of the running movement, the period during the 1970s when physical fitness and a public-facing private life became entwined. For more than forty years, then, a tradition has developed—if not an attitude, if not a standpoint—for listening-while-running.

The least charitable way to look at running, including my own running, is that it is selfish and anti-communal. The least charitable way to look at earphone-listening, including my own, is that it is a self-protective activity, a sort of narcotic or border wall. If running-while-listening has not been written about much, it may be because it does not seem pure of spirit. If running is a kind of diversion, and earphone-listening is a kind of diversion, then running-while-listening is a double-diversion, tens of millions of people in preening daydreams. I like some of the theories I've read about how music has evolved according to external, nonmusical factors—for instance, the English writer Valerie Wilmer's assertion that the difference in feeling between free jazz in New York City and Chicago had to do with skyscrapers and a tighter, hemmed-in city grid versus a relative sense of sprawl and open space. Or the Japanese musician Seigen Ono's theory that the booming, gated-reverb drum sound of mid-1980s pop had to originate in Europe and not Japan, because it mimics an echo off stone structures. (Whereas Europeans had centuries of experience of hearing sounds reflected off stone houses along both sides of roads leading in and out of their villages, Ono explains, Japanese villages had no stone structures; Japan was a "paper-and-wood culture.") In any case: Did the early Walkman give rise to its own music—music inspired by this new kind of listening?

It's certainly possible, and would be a music of its own because, generally speaking, listeners in the early 1980s already had several ways to listen to music; the Walkman was not their only or primary means of listening. But one can only guess what that music might be. The Cars, maybe. "Moving in Stereo," and the rest of their first album, was like audiophile music for kids who didn't have their own home stereo systems. Bands from the New Romantic movement—Ultravox, say—might have been Walkman music. Stirring, performative, crazily impetuous human-machine music. The sorts of sounds that intensify the feeling now known as main-character syndrome, but with the new assistance of synthesizers and digital rhythm. Listen to this music with earphones clamped on and you are a human avatar. Reap the wild wind!

I'm not convinced that earphone music is its own category. If I am looking for the solitary chill—I hear what I am, I am what I hear, and nobody else needs to know or understand—I can get that by listening to Bach's piano Partitas played out loud on a living room stereo, or even on a kitchen radio. The tenderizing force that makes me feel attended to, or even diagnosed, is in the music and the performance of it, not in the equipment.

But when the listener is moving, the question of one's evolving relationship to the music can become intensified.

I am fifty-five and I teach college students. Every year I give them an assignment involving a soundwalk—once a specific practice formulated by R. Murray Schafer and Hildegard Westerkamp, now a generic term for a walk in which the walker-listener is given directives to listen in a particular way, or toward a particular source of sound. I send the students a link to a randomizing soundwalk generator, developed by Stephanie Loveless and Brady Marks. I don't know how many different soundwalk prompts the generator can generate, but I'm not supposed to. The idea, for the walker-listener, is that you don't know what it's going to give you. One, for example, is called "Indeterminate Soundwalk":

1) Begin walking, begin listening.
2) Allow yourself to follow the most rhythmic sounds you can hear.
3) Consider: listening through your skin.
4) Continue your soundwalk longer than you feel like.

The students enjoy the exercise of taking the soundwalk and then writing about it, or at least they have a lot to say about it. Some are provocatively unimpressed. Some are moved or humbled. Some find themselves strangely obsessed with a new attunement to sonic stirrings in their neighborhoods that they hadn't noticed before. Some are disturbed by the experience of being out among strangers in a place that they had not themselves elected to go to: various soundwalks tell you to walk toward a body of water, or to step onto a subway or bus. Non-male students, in particular, are put slightly at risk by the assignment. At least one will come back with a story about how a harasser or an unbalanced person interfered with an otherwise positive experience.

But the main reaction is the novelty of moving through a public space, alone, without earphones on. Most of them—I don't mean some; I mean most—never walk alone without them. Increasingly, my students have made the investment of buying noise-canceling earphones and wearing them every time they go out to walk, sometimes every time they ride a bicycle. Normally they listen to music through the earphones, but just as often they don't. Their earphones signal to the city world that they don't want to be bothered; the earphones make them appear unreachable. And as the earphones superimpose the private soundscape they prefer over the public one that is forced upon them, they feel protected or otherwise helped. Some say the music counteracts the rest of the noise in their heads, or their ungrounded anxiety. Some say they are easily bored, and because walking can be boring—especially a purely functional walk, one done every day—the music helps make the day more colorful.

I'm not surprised by any of this. I'm sometimes surprised by the passion and vehemence they have about using earphones while walking in New York: to do otherwise, to them, can seem foolish or ill-advised.

Moving with music delivered straight into one's ears is, for many of the people who are shaping this world, more normal than moving with one's ears uncovered. But what I don't hear from my students very often is the idea that moving with earphones on can be a choice made specifically in order to go deeper into the music. In other words, they're often talking about music as insulation from the world, rather than talking about music as a world in itself.

I think they talk this way because they have learned that older people will disapprove of the fact that they are walking around with earphones on all the time, and they'd better have an inarguable response to the disapproval. They're right. You can hear it in my writing: I'm sizing them up, even as I am learning from them. If they characterize listening as armor, as a defense against a world that is hostile to them, which it is, then I'll understand that they're bracing themselves against the force of the world that older people—me—have made for them.

Usually, I don't have earphones on as I walk through New York. I would prefer to be aware as I make each calibrated step. So many attitudes come toward the walker, so many languages, so many different cycles of a day. Attitudes are not aligned. It's not as if everyone is walking to work at 8 a.m. and walking home at 5 p.m. Attitudes, hungers, anxieties, needs, enthusiasms converge in a series of tornadoes that follow the walker everywhere. There is no "we" in the city; there isn't much shared perception.

However, I run with earphones—usually away from crowds, often in urban wilderness, but still. I can't say that running with earphones is advisable. I'm missing something, probably a lot. I'm replacing what is given to me with what I choose.

A significant portion of the composer Annea Lockwood's practice has been recording the sound of water in various rivers: the Hudson, the Housatonic, the Danube. Some of these recordings have been organized into sound installations, including the voices of people who live near the water. (There are ten different languages spoken along the Danube.) Some have been organized into records. Sometimes, through textual notations, she provides information about exactly where and when and under what conditions the recordings were made. She has been clear that these sonic artifacts, like the record *A Sound Map of the Danube*, are not environmental documentation for the future. She is also pretty clear about not calling them music. And that may be why, though I love to listen to the river recordings, I don't listen to them while running. I've tried it, but for moving I prefer suggestions of motion made by humans. I run with the part of her work that codes to me as music, because it shows her hand more, through her manipulations of tape recordings and instructions for musicians.

She is cheerily resolute in her belief that people need sound just as much as people need, say, water, and that as "pure" sounds go, certain natural sounds are at least as complex and interesting as those made by humans, like sine-wave tones. She is an advocate for moving through the world without earphones on. But she also realizes that people do move through the world with earphones on. In a public interview about fifteen years ago, she talked about the purpose and strategies of *A Sound Map of the Danube*, and she also talked about mobile life with earphones. Here is some of what she said:

> Acoustic ecology is a vital development right now, and [there is] a recognition that we may not have to use our ambient environment to navigate physically to the same degree as human beings have had to do at various times in various places. But we need to be aware of it. That, combined with . . . I suspect re-recognition that sound, as I've thought

for so long and experienced and lived for so long, that sound is an *absolutely primary form of nourishment.* And at first I looked at iPod wearers as divorcing themselves . . . creating an alternative sonic reality in response to the rising levels of urban noise, just *noise.* But, more recently, I've thought that's part of it, and . . . that people are tapping into—that experience . . . sound waves flooding through the body—as an essential form of nourishment, like food. And I'm glad to see it now!

// 12 //

I am listening to Georg Philipp Telemann's *Twelve Fantasias for Transverse Flute Without Bass*, played by Barthold Kuijken. I'm running around southwest Yonkers, and the music is making me pay attention to my footfalls—they're not quite the same on the left and the right, each one accompanying the other.

It seems to me that a lot of baroque music—and to some extent music in general—depends on either of two related desires on the part of composer or musician, which are then mirrored and reenacted within the listener.

One is the desire to repeat an action you have done in order to feel it was done thoroughly, much as you might find more and more viable raspberries on a bush as you pick over it; or much as a person—a certain type of person—rephrases an argument many times in order to finesse a point, to be heard by another person completely, to finish scratching the itch of communication.

The other is the desire to look at an action you have done, or someone or something you have a relationship with, from a *different angle*. Different angles increase the subject's value. The more pictures of a piece of land that are made available to prospective buyers, the better the chance of selling the property. The more points of view that a biography represents—the more sources and interviews it contains—the more readers will trust it.

These two related desires aren't about correcting a mistake;

they are about needing new versions of beholding, until the thing being beheld drifts loose from its specific shape and function and scale and starts to seem almost magically important. A great deal of baroque music is "through-composed"—set down from beginning to end as a unified whole—but in a way that can seem not through-conceived. It begins with the theme—an event, something made out of nothing—and then moves into variations on that theme: revisions, repatternings, new beholdings of the theme, until the composer and the music and you all go together into an uncertain future, toward a vanishing point. The music is exciting to the extent that it seems to come from pushing forward relentlessly, beyond what can be predicted.

A friend recommended this music to me two years ago, but I haven't given it a proper listen until today. I take it up and run with it. With these solo pieces, Telemann built ever-greater musical structures for revision, finding the new angle, the alternate history. Those structures could seem to defy logic or lung capacity: in the second movement of the flute fantasias, he wrote a fugue, which incorporates at least two voices, for a monophonic instrument—like one person re-creating both sides of a conversation. Generally he moves statement by statement, lending us many possible views of each statement. This thoroughness may be all a listener can use to apportion their judgment; it is the sum of what many of us can enjoy and respond to. "Good job," we might think, nodding at Telemann. "What a high number of revisions you have there. You've really been pretty thorough. You've really thought it through."

Where does the music's excellence reside? Is Telemann writing a narrative or something that goes beyond narrative, like a tendency? Is the primary statement before all the revisions a kind of perfection, or is it only the roughest of rough drafts? Is the piece about Telemann making for himself a better hearing of the statement? Or is it about Telemann letting listeners feel that they are getting a better hearing of the statement? Is it about the practice of trial and error in order to reveal the innermost beauty of the statement? Is it about asking better questions? Does the desire in this music move toward perfection or unknowability?

I sense this: by revisiting, by restating with a difference, Telemann is making value. Barthold Kuijken, recording these pieces in a Belgian church with a nicely limited echo, is transmitting that value pretty faithfully. Not selflessly—he's part of it—but with great attention to tone and consistency and thoroughness. The more I run on these long, slow curls of hills and basins, the more attached I become to what I see, and the more valuable it is to me. I know that by being on the move, I have seen grim neighborhoods and scrubby parkland in startling conditions of light and at angles that I would otherwise never register. The value I confer on what I see by running is forceful; it seems to me there's nothing to argue about there. More running creates more value. Cynical, violent city planning and disregarded parking lots generally depress me, as they do many people. But seen on the go, they can appear dignified—not fascinating problems, but at least enlivening ones. This might be because, from many angles, I am seeing the ongoingness of them, and the necessity of perseverance.

I will have to edit all I have written here. Nothing I write is any good until I rake it, turn it over, leave some of it bumpy, wash it in rays of concern and fretting and curiosity, like Mal Waldron and Telemann. Even after I'm done, I see ways it can be better every time I happen to look at it.

// **13** //

Track three on *Les Tambours Du Mali*, by a four-part Malian drum ensemble led by Mamadou Kanté: a Wassoulou N'Gri rhythm, a beginning in 6/8 time at a slow-running pace.

The first drummer begins so unassumingly, delaying each stroke by a decisive millisecond: bim-*bim*-boom / bim-*bim*-boom-boom. You hear four bars of this, allowing you to respect the whole expanse of the six-beat rhythm; he doesn't seem to love any part of it less than any other part.

Then you hear four whole bars of the second drummer, whose job is to tip the scales toward the first half of the bar, making it sound *one*-two-three, *one*-two-three; then you hear four whole bars of the third drummer, adding another pattern that balances the first two, so they don't sound as if they're fighting. And then a star appears, making his splashy power entrance before four bars of the third drummer have finished. Maybe it's Kanté—I'm not sure.

While the first three maintain this capacious moving puzzle in wet lumps of sound, a rhythm made in compound, non-uniform work, the fourth distinguishes himself in dry, fast runs. He is ablaze, exciting. He is the soloist. But I have a question almost as soon as he appears: Is he the leader? Is he making the others sound good, or are the others making him sound good?

The tempo increases. The soloist dazzles in quick bursts, then stops, letting time elapse before he comes down hard in two-handed compound slaps that sound like *ploum*, a bit like what trap-set drummers call a flam, free-forming all his shapes and emphases while the other three keep their heads down, maintaining the structure. After three and a half minutes, the tempo very, very slowly begins to increase even more, until it reaches sprinting levels, and the lead drummer finds apotheosis; his power is unreachable, unthinkable. I sense him beginning to sweat, and I begin to think, "Oh no: what if he can't keep up?"

The last minute or so belongs to the first three drummers. The foundation becomes the house; the ground becomes the figure. They are repeating a fast rhythmic loop together, executed so regally that the lead drummer can add only small dots and strokes to their achievement. It is possible to think this is an example of a teacher empowering their students, letting them take over; a leader or a boss training junior workers; a parent emboldening children to do the job of growing and superseding, executing their soft mutiny.

The first two-thirds of the track resembles the thrill of holding, and the last third resembles the satisfaction of letting go. That shift generally happens a bit earlier for me in a run—it might happen in the first third. But in that shift a runner forgets about whatever discomfort and internal arguments it took to get into motion, to start moving, to push past resistance in the body or knots in the mind. The band has become a kind of self-generating system now, and the body responds in kind, feeling minimal strain amid all that balance. It's unclear whether the body has taken over from the mind, or the mind has taken over from the body, but since so much regarding the function of the body and the mind is a construct anyway, does it matter?

o

As I listen, here is the listener I propose: someone who is theoretically interested in everything, and not disappointed when
that interest dims; a discerner learning to question the terms
of their discernment; someone trying to know less so they can
know more. I generally gravitate toward what I still don't quite
understand, or the kind of music that makes me think, "What is
this?" or "Why is this?"—which could be, say, dance music, but
more often is music made outside commercial interests, or made
within a limited commercial structure.

I have become a little less interested in "works" of music, distinct and non-repeating and therefore easy to sell; I like the idea
of open systems, self-generating, ongoing, and shareable. Larry
Neal wrote in 1969 about the jazz saxophonist Pharoah Sanders:
"Pharoah has become one long beautiful song." I like the idea of
becoming the song, but also I have more and more time for long-
song makers. Someone who is said to make "the same record
over and over" is all right with me. If all music is intended as a
gift, I tend to spend more time listening to the gifts for which I
have not yet worked out a proper response as a recipient, because
those are usually the gifts I didn't know I wanted.

I tend to understand music starting from rhythm—repetition,
a drum, a rhythm section—and then upward into melody. (If
I come to understand the music nonhierarchically, as a unified
plane, that understanding comes later.) From time to time, I listen to something I know very well, but essentially I always want
to get somewhere new with it, somewhere that is elsewhere. I
do not particularly want to listen in order to put myself back
into some memorable time of peace or impressionability—when

I was, say, riding the bus to high school, or learning how to use the hot and powerful dishwasher at my first job, or at a baseball game with my grandfather in Ohio. I've heard a lot about this stance of listening, the nostalgic one, but I can't pull it off myself. If I listen to honor the past, my conscience warns me, I might stay there and never return.

o

So much public land is padlocked that I have to reroute for comic lengths—running under a noisy bridge, being denied entry to the next section of parkland, running back under the noisy bridge, making a U-turn to another lane, running under the noisy bridge again. It's like a sequence in an action movie in which the characters, boringly, must be seen moving from point A to point B, leaving it to the sound and image editors to make it interesting. *Les Tambours Du Mali* makes it interesting with another track, a two-drummer Dogon dance rhythm that stays cold and steady for five minutes, never flashing up into anything dramatic. This is the definition of taking the long way to go a short distance, but as I internalize how the drummers work, I don't mind at all.

I pass the butch, lovely track stadium at the south end of Van Cortlandt, a Works Progress Administration project built in 1939, during a different period of mass unemployment. I've never been on the track. Let's try it. The change from dirt and rocks and roots, cracked pavement and jagged direction to the soft, synthetic, rust-colored surface and perfect oval motion feels like a whole new sensory consciousness, like switching from one machine to another in an arcade.

Back to the Parade Ground for one more go-around, past the

spectator's reviewing stand. A group of women called Female Fight Club, who had been members of a nearby gym until it closed, exercise with weights on the viewing stand, at a suitable distance from one another. One of the police cars that have begun to slowly, symbolically patrol the park stops in front of the women. Both cops open their doors and make their authoritative, symbolic what-do-we-have-here walk from the vehicle toward the women: a duo approaching an orchestra, but there is more to it than that, given that they are non-Black cops approaching mostly non-White women. The cops have nothing better to do and express curiosity about joining the exercise group. They start jumping on and off the first row of the stands, feet together, imitating others in the group. First, the women cautiously accept them. Then they encourage them.

// 14 //

The New York City recordings of Bessie Jones during 1961 and 1962, talking and singing, form a field of their own: twenty-one sittings, fifty hours. Records have been made from them, but it is unclear how to think about them—as individual artifacts, as a corpus, or as something grander and more inconclusive, like an invitation or a reminder. Some songs are Bible stories or games—Bessie Jones said she knew "a hundred games," and she often called them "plays." Others call and warn and witness and fantasize. In most of the recordings, she sings alone, tapping her foot or clapping. In "Diamond Joe," the narrator finds herself in trouble: "Diamond Joe, you'd better come and get me. . . . My britches torn, I got no patches. . . . I'm out of dough and I got no clothes. Want to go home but I can't go." In "Gator," the narrator dreams of going away, making money, and bringing a feast back to his woman: "I'm gonna get me a gator, oh, gals / that big bold gator, oh gal." In "You Ought to Get Tired Sometime," she is disapproving: "I met my sister this morning / I shake her righteous hand / But before that day was over / she scandalized my name." All the songs are for passing the time, giving the world a charge or making it exciting, and creating motion with limited means: the Georgia Sea Island tradition she learned from used no band instruments.

Jones ran through her memories and songs in the folklorist

Alan Lomax's apartment, on West Third Street in Manhattan, right next to what is now a nightclub called Groove. The sessions were recorded by Lomax's wife, Antoinette Marchand, if "sessions" is the right word.

Jones already knew Alan Lomax, and Alan Lomax probably already knew some of the songs. Both Jones and Lomax wanted to be repositories and sharers, storers and transmitters, to fulfill different senses of duty. Her step-grandfather, Jet Sampson, had been born in Africa, taken into slavery in America as a child, and died at the age of 104; in her childhood he taught her many songs, stories, and movements. She was raised in central Georgia, where she began minding the children of others at age ten. By age twelve she had a husband, a child, and full-time work: imagine how desperately a preteen, impatient even without a baby, would have wanted to keep her day amusing while taking care of her own baby and others' babies, to recount stories and sing and keep things moving. When she moved to St. Simons Island in her thirties, she joined the Spiritual Singers Society of Coastal Georgia; she organized to keep a culture from disappearing; and then she was "called to teach." Lomax had first traveled to St. Simons Island in 1935 with two other folklorists, Mary Elizabeth Barnicle and Zora Neale Hurston, but Lomax didn't meet Jones until he returned in 1959 to make more recordings, by which time she had become a primary member of the island singers.

When Bessie Jones arrived at Lomax and Marchand's apartment in 1961, she stayed for three months; she wanted Lomax to record her life story and collect some of the songs and stories she knew, so that she could begin a proper career as a singer. Surely she sensed that the time was right: America had never before that moment cared in a serious way about the history of its own music, and the commercial apparatus of recording and performing was eager to cater to that new interest. These recordings were for reference—for possible books, for documentation to help her get work teaching and performing—and for posterity; they were not meant for public consumption. Anyway, the songs are not necessarily the point. Around the songs, she talks. She tells riddles and tongue twisters and gives toasts, talks about death, dancing, love, prayer, abortion, hauntings, early telephones.

Listening to these songs while running—the singing is quiet, built of repeated refrains—I think I can hear Lomax and Marchand listening to Bessie Jones and according a shape to all the songs and stories and humor and manners within her. The recordings go all the way around her sound and her voice. They pay attention to her in the present, and they generally have time for her. She doesn't need to shout and she doesn't need to hurry: Lomax and Marchand and their microphone hearken to her. The assumption spread by the hearkening is very simple: what Bessie Jones has to sing and say has great value and must be shared. Her inflections in "Gator" are like colors in the evening sky: they have no need to make an argument for themselves as such.

These recordings don't issue an explicit invitation to be listened to. Jones does not extend herself to you in the most efficient ways, and there is no sense of completion about them when they're done. If you want to listen to them, today, you have to figure out your own way through them: in a sixty-song collection called *Get in Union*, which I have with me as I run, or in streamed files in the Lomax Digital Archive. At the same time, Jones's reason for singing was plain and real: she was a designated storyteller of her people who decided to trust the intentions of these White people who wanted to help her preserve her stories. When she talks, she is often leading toward a song. When she sings, she is generally leading toward more talking, explaining what the song is about, because she would be content, it seems, to talk forever, and this work of collecting what she knows, as well as the work of educating White people, may never be done, and the recording's inbuilt forward motion matches a desire to keep running.

o

It might be helpful if there were a distinction between an act of art or design that purports to be finished, and one that is perhaps not hostile to, but simply uninterested in, the state of finishedness. Better still if the first is not necessarily better than the second.

A public park is a work of design. It is a system created with intention and proportion, to effect a sense of visual and spatial harmony. The harmony can be rendered by a land designer during the genesis of the park, or it can be rendered in stages and realized only later, through the will of the individual user of the park to experience harmony.

In 1875, the president of New York's Department of Public Parks, William Martin, recommended hiring Frederick Law Olmsted, the landscape architect who had designed Central Park and Prospect Park, to conceive an overall street map for the west Bronx, including the land that is now Van Cortlandt Park. Olmsted's plans turned out to be un-Manhattanesque: they were not based on a grid system, and they let the unruly terrain of the area, full of rocks and hills and unevenly shaped parcels, dictate the flow of the roads. For that reason, Olmsted's plans seemed to the Parks Department commissioners to be anti-commerce as well. (Grids are closed systems; grids are commerce.) Olmstead worked on the plan for three years. He recommended that the Parks Department purchase the Van Cortlandt property, and then he was taken off the project. So ended, more or less, the great New York park designer's affiliation with Van Cortlandt Park.

Most Manhattanites never travel to Van Cortlandt Park, but it is bigger than Central Park by half. The park had no defining architect. Its structure came about in phases, all of them designed for reasons of commerce and efficiency, none of them coordinated. (The park's structure is ongoing, but no longer for reasons of commerce or efficiency.) The Van Cortlandt family estate lay at its heart because it was already there; accordingly, the city drained a large field to create the open Parade Ground for military shows, the first of which occurred in 1884. In 1888 the Parks Department purchased the estate and its surrounding area— 1,146 acres, which would become known as Van Cortlandt Park. A few years later came the building of the Croton Aqueduct and the Putnam Railroad, forming two vertical stripes down the middle of the park. In 1895, the country's first public golf course was constructed in the southeastern quadrant. During the middle of the twentieth century, three multilane highways cut the park into four parts, which have never been meaningfully reconnected.

And so at this point, if you want to experience visual and spatial harmony in Van Cortlandt Park, you might have to make it yourself. A pathway for cyclists from the southern to northern end of the park was only recently built; its construction had stuttered for twelve years, facing opposition by conservationists. "Moving through the park" is not possible from east to west for walkers or cyclists. The divisions created by the highways are too profound.

In 1986, the New York City Parks Department hired a firm called Storch Associates to assess improvements to Van Cortlandt Park. "Access from perimeter streets is inadequate and poorly marked," they wrote.

> Once within the park there is neither an interconnected system of roadways nor a signage vocabulary to direct new guests. Those roadways which still exist are remnants of a historical road system which had been developed before the construction of the arterial highways and parkways, which later created barriers to the prior internal circulation. . . . Paths and walks within the park are frequently confusing, not located in response to desire lines, deadended by boulders, and not continuous from one area of the park to another.

A desire line is an unplanned route or path, worn by walkers, bikers, and runners, made not out of antipathy to an established or official path but out of simple indifference to it. (Sometimes it is made by intention rather than desire.) It is a kind of beneficent scar through a landscape.

I could live my whole life in my neighborhood without having any reason to go to Woodlawn, the principally Irish neighborhood next to mine. It lies just across the park, two miles away in a straight line, but I have to counteract a parkway and a state highway to get there, and so the line of my desire remains undrawn unless I choose to draw it. The only way I could draw it would be by following a network of trails that are not particularly meant to connect, and that were not ever meant to connect in anyone's finished plan.

Van Cortlandt Park is not a closed system, in that it isn't finished. But neither is it "open" by design. The running one can do in it amounts to a series of inscriptions suggested by its not-closed system. Those who use it are remixing it, or creating uses for it that couldn't have been intended by its creators. And those who use it are, of course, notching it along the way with whatever significance and value they attach to certain places at certain times. In this way it becomes an extension of them.

When running, I am alive to signs and symbols and warnings, I experience deep shifts of light and color and air pressure, I recognize patterns, I problem-solve; these processes become a counterpoint to my listening. And when I run and listen, I am taking in and retaining sounds, sights, physical sensations, and ideas at all times, such that I might clock a rhythmic disposition or a rhetorical problem or a smell or an earthen contour or a skyline shape, and thereafter I will keep noticing it in the world in other forms, including in music.

Practiced carefully, this activity based on listening and flowing forward will do as a way of drawing a different near future. (I mean very near: the future that starts at the vanishing point in my line of vision, and at whatever I would call the point in my line of listening when my predictive ability breaks down.) After all, the music is changing me, and I am changing it: I am creating conditions for it, and a context for it, that its makers hadn't anticipated.

Running can be an act of connecting physical zones—neighborhoods, terrains—that for one reason or another have been kept apart, as is the case in my area of the Bronx. The running can create a psychological version of desire lines: another way of imagining a future. Finally, running—with or without listening—can involve a crucial element of future-making: the opportunity for a sudden variation on an established pattern. At the moment of their highest, most impetuous creativity, runners can shake loose from whatever they have come to expect of themselves and become the person they will be tomorrow, simply by turning in a different direction. You can always make it home by coming back around—unless you encounter people who try to stop you. (They might. You might represent some kind of disorder. Because, to a certain way of thinking, who needs to run but the guilty, the fearful, the critical, or the haunted?)

o

I am in Van Cortlandt Park most days, and I enjoy its design, to the extent that there is one or that I make one. The best plan is to be like Bessie Jones in her recording sessions and think of my running sessions as indistinct, never finished. In this way I draw my own desire lines—or intention lines—in the park, which makes it far more than a work of design. It becomes a unit of time, of space, of light, and of air. It is the measurement of what I can see on a level plane, and of how far I am traveling. It is, in a sense, my watch, my odometer, my color spectrum, and my barometer. If I let it, it can be my DJ and my conductor.

// 15 //

Awake in the dark with the terrors of the season, I think: "A good plan, any plan, will send me back to sleep. What will I listen to while I run in the morning?"

For a little while I have been following the trail of complex or frenetic or disorienting music, or music with many centers. Eric Dolphy, the Malian drummers, Don Cherry and Ed Blackwell. What if I choose music that has only one center, that is generally known to make you stay put, and that many are happy to leave on in the background? What about Sade?

Recently I heard Sade's *Love Deluxe* for the first time. I had heard nearly half its contents—there were four radio hits from the album in 1992—but I mean the whole album, in sequence. Where was I in 1992? Not listening to pop music, I guess. None of my friends called me on the telephone and told me I had to stop whatever I was doing and listen to the Sade record. So it's both familiar and not familiar. It'll work.

Running is a combination of flying and tracking—the way one launches into a free-from-Earth *praeceps* flight, and the way one grips the furrow. The word "engagement" amounts to a metaphor for that grip—the treads of your shoe engaging with the dirt or the road—but it can also be a metaphor for flight. It takes concentration and purpose and "engagement" to stay aloft and hurtling ahead. You are halfway in the air, or—I am picturing the warning lights just outside radio-station control rooms—"on air." You are in session.

So much is determined by tempo in this music. Sade Adu's voice has a strong subjective conscience: it is a wave of self-possession. The ur-Sade tempo settles at around eighty-five beats per minute—rather slow, not necessarily ballad-slow, but on the low end of what might be considered mid-tempo. Many hit songs that aren't ballads have been made in that range—soul music is full of this tempo—but most of those songs are merely using it, backing into it; Sade *is* it. Can this tempo be considered a running tempo? Not according to runners' magazines. One hundred twenty to one hundred forty beats per minute, they say, is best for running, or up to one hundred sixty for "pushing yourself." I can't stand runners' magazines. Here is a moment to question what "pushing yourself" means.

Sade can make a runner fly, conscientiously. "No Ordinary Love" works as a running song: its atmosphere is tense, its drumming steady, serious, and minimal, drawing your attention to small events, such as the three displaced backbeats before Sade sings the title phrase. Even "Like a Tattoo," track four, a love song with no drums (only voice, guitar, and piano), can move a runner on the strength of its conviction.

"Cherish the Day," track six: a touch slower than "No Ordinary Love," even graver in its intent. Let me stay with this song for a minute. In my youth when I worked for a book publisher, I remember attending an editorial meeting with a man who wanted to publish a book of candid photographs of Elvis Presley that he'd collected. I was amazed by the number of them he had. He'd really put his back into it: many years of work there. I said something to him like "You've really got a lot of photographs." He looked at me with a grave face. "This is a lifetime situation," he replied. Funny story, but it wasn't funny at the time. This man had no funny moves. He wanted to communicate, but he could talk about only one thing. He wanted the full hearkening.

What I missed by not hearing *Love Deluxe* in full in 1992 is the degree of involvement a listener can reach by the point of "Cherish the Day." That, surely, is part of Sade's gift as a singer and a bandleader—her ability to deliver music that looks at a distance very much like a commodity, but that close up becomes a lifetime situation. Which is to say, she has only one thing to impart, which is the aesthetic and physical presence of Sade in the world, and she is not going to be distracted by any other subject. She trusts her own favored modes and timbres and doesn't fill in the empty spaces with virtuosity. So she teaches you how to listen: she establishes the parameters for you to take her seriously. And what is the first line of this love song? "You're ruling the way that I move."

That's pretty close to what I have been looking for: a way to describe how one can move and be moved within the specifications of another person's music. On many days I want to move the way Ed Blackwell plays; I like to feel I am moving with him cooperatively, and am happy to follow his lead. But on this day, and many days in the future, I will want to move something like the way Sade sings. The logic of "Cherish the Day" is mirror-image first person: within the song, she is essentially saying, "Let me tell you about something that someone has done to me," but the effect of the song is about her doing that precise thing to you.

I feel bereft when the song ends, and can't find my footing in "Pearls," the track that follows, but my struggle doesn't have anything to do with that song per se; I've had too much of a good thing. So much that I need to start walking. But that's all right.

// 16 //

I decide to run with Mal Waldron some more: *Impressions*, from 1959.

Why Mal Waldron again? Because he worked the same ideas over and over, not even from day to day but in one solo; because he was a prince of repetition; because the repetition needed not have a plan or a moral, other than what it embodied so well that an explanation was unnecessary. I imagine many artists and writers have dreamed of a direct route to people's minds and bodies, a way to jab their audience not with an idea or something with a point, but with a complete disposition or a way of looking at the world. Mal Waldron does this. I'm not quite sure why I never noticed this well enough. As I pass the James J. Peters Department of Veteran Affairs Medical Center on Sedgwick, heading south toward Devoe Park, I listen to "Ciao!," a detonating unaccompanied piano introduction, then a kind of fast Bud Powell–like trio theme ending in a tiny glimpse of Powell's "Parisian Thoroughfare," then the long section where Waldron solos over the bass and drums. It's an altered blues form, steering into clouds of repetition; his solo blooms in the middle of the track, sending an idea through slight permutations as the rhythm grooves along; at one point he strikes the same dissonant chord maybe thirty times in a row; he's operating within the structure of a discrete chorus of a song, but he moves you past the point when you wonder where he'll come out, so the idea of a song with a beginning and end becomes disrupted. He's-doing-something becomes what-is-he-doing? The song moves strong and fast, that's for sure; he's just temporarily refusing to show that he's in a song. In any case, his playing doesn't represent a poised ideal of storytelling or a representation of anything else, but it's what he's doing for his circumstances, in 1959, in a room with microphones, on the clock. His playing accepts motion as an idea in itself.

In other words: if his music doesn't seem calibrated toward pointed narrative relevance, he understands the ways in which persevering *is* narrative relevance. Moving the left leg and then the right leg is a lot and is enough.

I am paying such close attention to Mal Waldron because he can be exciting, to a point, but more than that because in his music he is wary, he is acknowledging the complexity of saying anything at all, he puts the complexity right there on the surface; he isn't trying to pretend that life is simple. He is engaged and resigned at the same time. He will do this today and he will do this tomorrow. He won't give up, won't be denied. It's pretty hot, could be worse, but the air is dense, and the times are dense; there's a temptation to stop, but then again, why?

The ability to stay upright and engaged—as opposed to keeping silent, dying, or otherwise disappearing—deserves attention. Do it over and over again: that's the idea. Do it differently, with different inflections, with ease or in pain, outrageously or boringly, but just do it and become yourself. "Good" or "bad" as markers of the repetition will fall away after a while. The act will assume its own lesson and mark out a larger tendency. It will become great, if you like. Making art can be boring. Running can be boring. Asking the same questions can be boring. But now is a good time to ask the same impossible question day after day, in order to render the efficient answer inadequate. Whenever "boring" runs hot through intent or repetition, it becomes valuable.

○

Some windows have been broken and property has been damaged on Fordham Road. It's still tense there three days later. The presence of the police is felt, and distrust is ambient, like a metallic smell. People are irritable—muttering, but not into their phones; they are looking hard at others, including me. I slow down to a walk, take out my earphones, and pass a man staring ahead and thinking out loud as he passes a line of police. He's saying something. What's he saying?

You *needed* to win, . . . and so you won, motherfucker.

What the man says deserves to be heard and taken seriously. He might be saying it to me or to the cops. Or to both, or to neither.

Mal Waldron rumbles on. I rumble on. Three blocks north of Fordham Road, it is quiet and less tense.

He played romantic ballads known from romantic singers— like "All the Way," on this record—adding graceful passing chords as needed; and he played his own bumpy and repetitious songs. He was not cute—he didn't have that in him. He kept his mileage up, kept working, recorded hundreds of sessions, while doing things the way he wanted to do them. In the late '90s, while living in Brussels, he told me he didn't particularly want to perform in the States, because he couldn't smoke cigarettes in clubs any longer, and didn't express any regret about that. He didn't need to win. I also remember writing with doubt or confusion about his enterprise, reasoning that sometimes he was boring. I would like to revise that opinion. I now know that if you find something boring, it says more about you than about the thing— but then again, it is good to imagine him hearing this sort of response fairly frequently, staying in motion, and not allowing himself to be particularly bothered by it. There, again: to engage with someone's music while running might possibly—not assuredly but possibly—allow you to imagine certain triumphant aspects of being someone else. This engagement may be different from empathy in that it can apply only to someone else in a state of motion and not to a static perception of them.

// 17 //

I begin listening to Sofia Gubaidulina's first string quartet and notice first a trembling drone and then a lot of glissandi played apart and together in contrary motion, which taken together suggests circles, and which I interpret as circular motions pushing toward stark and unfamiliar places.

So without really thinking about it, I do something analogous to what the music does. I run down a hill into Kingsbridge, greeting the astonishing light, moving toward the light of the high, glassy, clustered chords, and then up a hill, crossing the valley of Broadway and going directly east as far as I can go: two hundred feet down to sea level and two hundred feet up again. I bump into the Jerome Park Reservoir, which is closed, but you can run around the whole thing on the empty streets, past ball fields and medical tents. A rough and giant circle to the other side, where the schools are, Bronx Science and Lehman College, curving back around on Sedgwick—alternating apartment blocks and freestanding houses with steps up to the front doors. Then back toward our neighborhood, via the Van Cortlandt Stadium, where I trace a couple more circles on the track.

o

Here is the writer I propose: a music critic who has become less and less interested in what the former standard modes of music criticism look like. I respect the notion of writing as work, and I respect my guild—an imaginary guild, because most critics don't acknowledge themselves as such, and tend to be shaky joiners anyway. I was trained in the unit of the record review, but I have some doubt about it now, because by and large I have doubt about the unit of the record. Something's changing. One can write about oneself in relation to the music, or to one's memory; one can write about a record's musicality and its tradition or system; one can write about issues of work or ethics or emotion around it; but the record itself as the boss—I'm less sure about that. The critic's task is to clarify. Clarify what, though?

It is not important for critics to establish a finite truth or absolute values. We don't need to win in that way. But we can move closer to clarity by means of questions, metaphors, descriptions, interpretations, and understanding the subject's origin and connections, none of which necessarily add up to what is understood as an opinion. An opinion is easy to spot when it's coming your way; a reader who thinks, "This isn't for me" simply moves out of the way, or wasn't within range of the opinion from the start.

I propose a knuckleball method. A baseball pitcher, throwing a knuckleball, puts their thumb on the bottom of the ball and digs into the top, clawlike, with their index and middle fingers. When they let go of the ball, they flick it forward with the index and middle fingers, creating a topspin to counteract the natural bottom spin that results from throwing any round, palm-sized object. The result is a ball that does not spin at all. Its fixed flight makes it susceptible to turbulence in the air. Thrown plainly, it lands strangely. (It is easier for a pitcher to throw a ball that spins, and the spin makes the ball more likely to reach its target.) Mal Waldron was a knuckleball artist. When possible, I would like to write in this hard way, without making the words spin, and not being too sure of how they will land.

Music is difficult to write about, for the simple reason that it must always be caught up with. Music moves from here to there; it is running away from us. The fact that it runs away from us is a source of joy but also of displeasure: a song can drive you crazy, or beguile you, or perplex you, or threaten you. For this reason, many ignore its motion, or are asked to, and write about music (or are asked to) as if it were a finite historical event, which has to mean something; it's better if that something can be sharpened to a weapon-like point. Much that has been written for a general readership about music—especially lately, and especially about pop, but not exclusively so—could have been written with the writer's having had access only to a lyrics sheet, a press release, and a transcript of an interview with the musician talking about the meaning and intent of their work, but not the actual music itself. I think there might be a double bind here. As I see it—by which I mean, as I hear it—the truth of music is in its motion. But as soon as a writer starts describing the motion of music, their editors and readers, even some who would prefer the truth, start to turn away.

It would seem to be worthwhile to acknowledge music's headlong identity, even if capturing it is impossible. The best writing about any art—and the best art too—is generally the kind that stretches toward the limits of its capabilities, and that points, at least, toward what a writer or an artist can't quite express.

○

Music runs away from us. Gubaidulina's does, manifestly. Half an hour into her third string quartet, I still don't know where it's going. The strings are prodding me, coming at me with invisible fingers—the fingers of the musicians, playing the pizzicato first half, gathering into masses and then dispersing. In the fourth string quartet, live strings are set against prerecorded sounds of a ghost quartet bouncing rubber balls against the strings, producing the effect of a quickly retreating echo. The string sounds and the musicians themselves are there and not there. What do we do with this music? We can *chase* it, but a chase implies we want to capture it, like a hunter chasing an animal, or that we want to know where it is going, like an officer chasing a suspect. I'm not sure that's the best response. We can also run roughly alongside it, allowing for it to move in any direction. We can listen to the song, dance to the song, collect the song, study the song, live by or represent the song. There is also always the option of running the song.

I see that if I go a little farther east next time, I will reach another WPA circle, the Williamsbrige Oval, near Gun Hill Road. I can think of a lot more music with circles in it. I might use more of Gubaidulina's, because I am in a mystico-Russian mode anyway, reading *The Brothers Karamazov*. I finally broke through its wall last night, pushing past the "Grand Inquisitor" poem and the endless last words of the Hieromonk and Elder Zosima. Now I can run faster through that book.

I'm aware that in this particular case I may be ignoring the "meaning" of the composer's music—if Gubaidulina would say its meaning is something to do with spirituality or the subconscious, though I don't know exactly what she would say. And whatever I did with the music today was not exactly musicology. But I wonder if I'm getting close to it, nevertheless, by running my discernment of it.

// 18 //

It's good to run with known music and an unknown path; or, as for most of today, with unknown music and a known path. The musician and producer Laurel Halo's new DJ set, called *Public Knowledge: Carrier Bag of Music*, which the term "DJing" doesn't describe very well, brims with short bits and pieces of sound and voice, sound sketches and field recordings and secondary matter that was apparently given to her by other musicians and producers. Like I do, she gathered ideas from her friends. Some of her friends are well-known, but this is a work of music whose intent is hard to identify, with no obvious heroic sequences. If you want to see which friends she included, you have to make a point of looking it up. Hers is one of several DJ sets inspired by Ursula K. Le Guin's nearly forty-year-old essay "The Carrier Bag Theory of Fiction." (Halo's set, and the others, were commissioned by a publisher who has just reprinted Le Guin's essay). The essay imagines a novel or a story as a bag of voices and ideas rather than as a weapon. A piece of cultural knowledge, Le Guin reasoned, is either one or the other. And the (circular, holding, gathering, admixing, multipurpose, less male-identified) bag predates the (sharp, single-purpose, results-oriented, hero-oriented and conflict-oriented, more male-identified) weapon.

Laurel Halo's bits and pieces don't add up to a grand statement or story. The set really amounts to a container more than a narrative. (So, too, does *Get in Union*, and any of the other records made from Bessie Jones's debriefings with Lomax and Marchand.) But the intent with which its contents were placed beside one another seems to become its own logic. It has some form—it has a beginning and end, and tensions and connections—but its quality of motion supersedes its quality of thingness or workness. There are some young amateur singers in a choir rehearsing their parts individually; a few readings of Taoist texts; solo guitar or wind-instrument arpeggios over beats; a woman reading a fascinating personal essay, though I don't know whose it is. As I run on paths near the Harlem and Hudson Rivers, on hilly roads and overgrown riverside paths, I can't gain a secure foothold in this music, but then again I don't particularly want to—I'll take whatever the set gives, because a cheerful fuzziness around narrative and provenance is in the spirit of the thing. Parts of the route I run while listening to Laurel Halo are quite steep—and parts are places where I have stalled out and walked in the past. But the lack of a steady beat isn't a problem. Curiosity sets a pace; it has a tempo.

o

Here is a passage from Haruki Murakami's book *What I Talk About When I Talk About Running*:

What exactly *do* I think about when I'm running? I don't have a clue.

On cold days I guess I think a little about how cold it is. And about the heat on hot days. When I'm sad I think a little about sadness. When I'm happy I think a little about happiness. . . . Random memories come to me too. And occasionally, hardly ever, really, I get an idea to use in a novel. But really as I run, I don't think much of *anything* worth mentioning.

I just run. I run in a void. Or maybe I should put it the other way: I run in order to *acquire* a void. But as you might expect, an occasional thought will slip into this void. . . .

The thoughts that occur to me while I'm running are like clouds in the sky. Clouds of all different sizes.

I'm glad he asked himself this question: What do I think about when I'm running?

When I mention to others that I am writing something about listening and running (and writing), most people who know me understand that I am not writing about endurance, speed, distance, pronation, heart rate, or other subjects related to sports, exercise, or science. And so most say, "I assume you have read Haruki Murakami's book?" It is one of the very few books on running not written for runners per se; and it is written by someone who knows a great deal about music—although musical thoughts take up only a very small part of the book. I am glad he wrote the book, and I have returned to it many times.

Murakami's writing can neutralize its own shortcomings as it moves along; that is part of its magic. He doesn't settle on any idea long enough either to let its interior complexity come out, or to expand it until he achieves integrative thinking. He writes about the experience of running a sixty-two-mile ultramarathon, for example, and the psychological "thin film" he felt subsequently wrapped in. He calls this film "runner's blues," perhaps because he appreciates the homeliness of commonplace ideas and has listened to a lot of blues. Then he seems to realize the limitations of the cliché; he finally defines the feeling as more milky white than blue. He tends to demur about what he has learned from it all—what an eviscerating and possibly radical experience sixty-two-mile marathon represents or leaves behind or generates for him or, in the reframing and retelling of it, for anyone else. He shrugs and essentially writes something to the effect of "I don't know," or "I don't have a clue."

For several reasons, I don't mind this tendency of his. One, he's evidently saving something for himself—he is maintaining a private life. Two, he's acting like his fictional characters, who do supernatural things and then think little of them. Three, he is refusing to be grandiose or special. Four, I myself like to say, "I don't know" when I don't know.

But I think there may be more to say beyond clouds and demurral. Running is often like a performance—you are imposing upon public spaces, moving through environments as if they were sections of a concert or a dance, flinging yourself on and through the world. Running is noncompetitive, soloistic, self-directed, quiet, and yet in a way it can represent the opposite of keeping to yourself. This may be the trouble with running through a graveyard. It is definitely the trouble with running through a neighborhood set on edge by a police occupation. Or through a subdivision with an active homeowners' association.

As for not having a clue what he thinks about as he runs: He means something, but what? The thoughts I have when I run are so clustered, unreasonable, and sometimes unsavvy, like the thoughts of someone's first day on Earth, that when I return to my desk and write some of them down, they look alien. But they clean my head, pushing out staleness. On a good day of running, which is most days of running, I don't acquire a void. I think I do the opposite of what he is talking about: I start with a void, or what I perceive to be a void, and then I start noticing thoughts. These thoughts are like comets—they can't be pinned down very easily. "Thought," as a noun, is probably the wrong word for them. A verb would do better.

Perhaps it is Murakami's emphasis on *training* that prevents him from developing broader ideas about running. The book, now that I'm looking at it again, is made up of essays written for running magazines—these assignments, and their particular audiences, are its origin—connected with free-writing exercises about his accomplishments and daily practices, and particularly the pleasure and pain involved in writing novels. I am wrong to say he does not write associatively about running. To be precise, he associates long-distance running with writing novels. He talks about the physical strain of writing, and he means it: He is irritated with the popular notion of writers being all brain and no body. He has a body and it often hurts. He seems to have a theory about a "toxin" carried by many writers—the heavy stuff with which they must wrestle, et cetera—and the necessity of physical training to keep the toxin in check, all for the purpose of prolonging productivity as a writer. He loves his systems and his productivity schedules; he likes to be busy. Clearly, he is describing a coping mechanism; clearly, there are things he would prefer not to think about. So perhaps he is also running from something! I might like to have an idea about what that is. I might also like to know what he is running toward. But as long as he comprehends running through the prism of numbers— "fitness," "health," "productivity" as nouns rather than verbs— maybe I never will.

When running becomes professionalized, eased, and supported by data and monitors, I imagine that it might no longer be philosophical. It becomes less of a proposition and more of a fact. I don't know if I have much desire to watch footage of recent marathons. But I have been enjoying the marathon portion of Kon Ichikawa's film about the 1964 Tokyo Olympics—particularly the difference between the stoic and measured performance of Abebe Bikila, the Ethiopian gold medalist, and other runners who seemed to bottom out well before the end, in their early-days running shoes (or in bare feet), after what was likely a pretty nonprofessional training regimen.

To become stuck in the task of writing, such that you can't move forward anymore, is terrifying. When you are young perhaps this stasis may take the form of a limited worry, but by the time you're in middle age, and consider yourself a "writer"—why else would you write seriously in middle age?—the inability to move forward in writing is a premonition of death. The reason for Murakami to be so preoccupied with writing novels at a steady pace—and writing, as he does in *What I Talk About*, about how much he looks forward to seeing what his next novel will be about—seems to be about staying alive. The great pianist and bandleader Eddie Palmieri told me, when he was sixty-five, that his major interest was "extending maturity and resisting decline." I suppose one way of doing this is to create big, blocky works of music, the kind that will lend you weeks and months of momentum, rather than short works that will quickly exhaust their mandate. I think Murakami's training reminds him that he can still engage with big projects, which to him signifies that he is still living. By running marathons, Murakami is essentially writing novels. Just as I am running songs to write music criticism. Amid some long tones, vocal and digital, in Laurel Halo's DJ set, I pass the assisted-living place and wave to the nurses and old fellas smoking outside it, enjoying their lungs, as I also am.

// 19 //

People are coming out a bit more. We go to a late-morning vigil on the Parade Ground, in front of the reviewing stand. The vigil proceeds in waves—it starts with several hundred people, several hundred more join, and so forth. While there, we are asked more than once to go down on one knee for more than eight minutes. It is a very long time. An unusually long period of time, too, these days, to be among a large crowd, still and listening.

A day later I run around the field and past the same area, eager to revisit it, to think about the rare sight of all the neighborhood people on the grounds, to remember the crowd's shape and how far it extended. I start with György and Márta Kurtág playing Kurtág's and Bach's piano pieces double-handed, to give myself something rigorous and unaccountable for the first few miles, and to take my mind off my sore feet. I can hear some of the outside world filtered through it, which I want, and when I listen to Kurtág's quieter solo piano pieces, "Preludium and Chorale" and "Hommage à Christian Wolff (Half-asleep)," the slight external hiss of wind around my earphones enters the musical arrangements.

I turn into the woods and switch over to the falsetto-voiced soul singer Eddie Kendricks, on the record of his I like best, for its buoyancy: the self-titled one. I don't only like it because of his voice, which suggests the opposite of the indelible—he makes love songs with light and imperfect sounds, destined to evaporate quickly. I like it also because the air that buoys his voice lives in the rhythm section too.

o

I've been thinking about Ahmaud Arbery's daily running practice in his part of southeast Georgia—a short drive across a causeway from Bessie Jones's St. Simons Island—which was to leave his mother's small house on a quiet suburban road in a mostly Black part of Brunswick; turn left; get out to the road; turn right. He ran for a couple of miles along Fancy Bluff Road, which is narrow, two-way; across some railroad tracks; past the First African Baptist Church, with four skinny columns out front; under the branches of many live oaks, shaggy with Spanish moss; then across Route 17, the causeway leading out toward Jekyll Island, and finally into Satilla Shores, an exclosure without fences, where mostly White and mostly older people live in ranch houses near the water. Route 17 is a kind of border. Arbery crossed a border—as runners often like to do in order to run connecting lines through a larger area, and in order to make a kind of song of their area—and then ran a loop through a subdivision, before coming back out again. It's a great route. I've looked at it online, followed it on Google Street View, partly to determine whether he was running from or running to—whether he was still running away from home or on the return leg—when he was killed. I can't quite figure it out, because at some point he might have changed directions while being chased at gunpoint by the local residents. If so, he did not change directions because he wanted to, which is the right and joy of runners; he changed directions because he had to.

I've been thinking about how my vantage point as a runner—how I see people and things while on the move—has come to determine my vantage point as a listener. (There is no adequate aural equivalent for "vantage point.")

To a certain way of thinking, I am seeing people at their best in the park where I run. If I can see them frontally, they generally have a short period for visually fixing me before I pass them; they have time to become comfortable with my shape and movements and appearance, and they compose themselves. Because I'm working at a task that has nothing to do with them, and will be gone in an instant, they're relaxed and open, or shy in the most lovely way of being shy. They tend to be over thirty: yes, they do. About half are Black. They have humored or pensive or resolute faces. They're not unlike people at a concert that seems so good it could be world-solving yet is "not for everyone": they're interested in who else might have come to it. By a standard friendship qualification—"Would I hang out with this person?"—I would hang out with nearly all of them, or at least I think I would when I'm on the move. I am seeing not just who they are, to the extent I can, but who they imply. In the places where I tend to run—parks and woods and trails and low-density streets—people walk alone or in twos; their inner lives beam out of them.

I also know, to take the bloom off the rose, that because I'm White, male, tall, straight, and middle-aged, I almost never interpret or experience those beams as a danger. Ahmaud Arbery wasn't so lucky.

It may be true that it is easier for me to like any of these fleeting people when our interaction is managed and limited—wordless, in fact—and when there is some careful, mutual apprehension, built on a respect for space: to begin with, they don't want me to run into them, and I don't want to run into them. But such is the nature of interactions on the go: they are short but deep, limited but positive.

O

When Eddie Kendricks sings "Can't Help What I Am," the song's conceit is about abdicating responsibility, not the kind of thing I enjoy celebrating lately, but there's more to it than that. His phrasing is conversational to the point of improvisation, and he manages that improvising in a pretty cut-and-dried pop song. I consider that whoever wrote these lyrics might have dictated them in one roll. "I believe," Kendricks sings, "somewhere there's someone / so much bigger than me, / and he's controlling the earth and the sun." Okay then: the concept is about going along for the ride, or playing along with it. Someone's leading his band. He is content to be carried, much as I am carried by listening to him, or sometimes by watching other runners. The narrator may be this very singer, the record may have his name on it, but he is not directing the action; he is tracing beautiful motions within the parameters he's been given. And over the upright groove, someone taps a rim or a metal bar with a thin wooden stick: it's a clanky feeling, almost casual or an afterthought, and for that reason rhythmically significant.

Frank Wilson was the arranger of this song (or the most prominent of several arrangers on this record, anyway). Why those decisions? Why that arrangement? The metal bar is a dazzling detail, not mixed high enough to become an irritant.

The run is now extending into a new chapter, a new neighborhood. I've threaded through the area by the park, where there are some fast-food restaurants, a sketchy hotel, and a middle-income apartment building that was recently the site of the largest heroin bust ever in New York State; then through a gas-station-and-bodega area of southwest Yonkers; and now I'm nearing some of the most expensive houses in the Bronx, once I get on the far side of the mountain. Meanwhile, the record remains agreeable, almost courtly, even as it does extraordinary things, even as it offers many elements to apprehend. The great mountain in its middle is "Keep On Truckin'"—its most complicated structure, with the most subsections and key changes, a series of changing atmospheres, a kind of prayer about perseverance. It expands and contracts and jumps among levels, moving through fields and lanes, a vibraphone part, a dip into an emptied-out plain and several new horn patterns, the terraces of the music switching places. It takes a very long time to do what it has to do. By the end of it, I feel invigorated and a little overwhelmed. Back at home, out of curiosity, I check to see how long that song is. Eight minutes.

// 20 //

The Joseph Haydn string quartets from Opus 20, which I am running with today, are committed to the principles of balance and forward motion and equilibrium. They seem to logically expand on these principles from the work of someone like Telemann, say, who published his *Twelve Fantasias for Transverse Flute* forty years earlier; here they spread outward into tonality, tradition, gesture, arrangement, mood. Major will be balanced by minor. Violin will be balanced by viola and cello. Country dance-energy will be balanced by fractal baroque precision. A gesture in the bass clef will be mirrored in the treble clef, just as in my listening every sudden step toward safety with the left foot through this scrubby, shaded, root-filled path—I've twisted an ankle here before—will be stabilized by the right. Nearly every one of Haydn's strong ensemble phrases is counterweighted by a delicate individual phrase. He doesn't leave anything disproportionate. It is music with high-level proprioception, conducive to running, bright and encouraging in its regularity, and sometimes not particularly exciting. Maybe it's a sort of Western standard for that which is cumulative, progressively circumspect, orderly, undisturbing.

The music is still profound, though. The first minute in the first movement of the quartet in D major, with its anchoring chords of low notes, repeated four times, creates a restful starting place, and it's maybe even "simple," but also secretly intense: the exhilarating mundane, to be quickly counterbalanced by shooting violin arpeggios. Just at this arrival of contrasts, the northbound Metro-North Hudson Line—close to where I am running—sidles up and then storms by for twenty seconds. I hadn't heard it coming. Elegant and brutal. Very simple. My running has connected Haydn to a train.

o

Murakami's quarter-page paragraph in an early section of *What I Talk About* amounts to about half of the book's music-related writing. "Sometimes when I run, I listen to jazz," he writes, "but usually it's rock, since its beat is the best accompaniment to the rhythm of running. I prefer the Red Hot Chili Peppers, Gorillaz, and Beck, and oldies like Creedence Clearwater Revival and the Beach Boys. Music with as simple a rhythm as possible." Strange from a man who organized his young adulthood around jazz records—he managed a bar in which they were ritually played and listened to—and knows more music from the classical tradition than I ever will, with the minute distinctions between performances and recordings that only a serious collector and listener can manage, but okay, he has a point: if "as simple a rhythm as possible" indicates a steady beat played with decisiveness, then yes, that can aid in the powerful and repetitive motion of running. But Murakami is not using the language of exhilaration. It seems he wants the music to do a job sufficiently well, and perhaps to make him feel comfort, as he performs his strenuous, maturity-extending, decline-resisting task—which again seems odd, because as an artist himself, he is presumably attuned to the problem of sufficiency. If he were merely sufficient as a novelist, we wouldn't read him.

Of course, the runner Murakami doesn't have to have the same relationship with music that the listener Murakami does, or the writer Murakami. There may be three different Murakamis, all adeptly managed by a higher part of his brain.

o

"No one can have an idea once he starts really listening," wrote John Cage, in his 1954 essay/lecture "45' for a Speaker." Susan Sontag elaborated on this idea, writing about looking in "The Aesthetics of Silence" thirteen years later:

> Silence is a metaphor for a cleansed, noninterfering vision, in which one might envisage the making of art-works that are unresponsive before being seen, unviolable in their essential integrity by human scrutiny. The spectator would approach art as he does a landscape. A landscape doesn't demand from the spectator his 'understanding,' his imputations of significance, his anxieties and sympathies; it demands, rather, his absence, that he not add anything to it.

To really listen, Cage and Sontag were both proposing, is to have your idea-machine disabled, to have no more room in your head for thought. These might be good arguments for running through a landscape without music. But Sontag might also be arguing for not entering a landscape at all. At any rate, I seldom run through her idea of a landscape—an unpeopled place. I tend to run where people have already been and left some kind of track behind. To do otherwise is to get your ankles twisted.

o

Reading, like running, helps connect the world, enables you to perceive one thing as growing out of another or responding to another, and in some cases reveals a knowledge within you that you didn't know you had. Italo Calvino wrote that a classic work of literature is "a book which even when we read it for the first time gives the sense of rereading something we have read before." Such was the case for me with "Field," and such is the case for me today with these Haydn string quartets: I don't know this music, though I feel I do, which is slightly different from being familiar with it. I think the gratefully reckless sensation of running, with minimal fear of twisting your ankles, can help push a listener toward the sense Calvino is describing.

I came across Calvino's quotation in a Moyra Davey essay about the problem of how to choose what to read—essentially, whether to read for knowledge or for thrill. She writes specifically about the kind of reading in which you allow a friend's recommendation to derail whatever you're in the middle of, and enable the Cage-like, chance-operations aspect of having your mind open to something unplanned, as if it were a snatch of something in the air. Relatedly, she allows her criticism to move and grow by accretion and instinct and chance, letting the reader in on her daily practice of putting her machine together. At this point I realize I have become attuned to passing sounds and blink-of-an-eye recommendations. I take up suggestions and stay moving. I'd like to try to encounter what I don't know, with just a slight promise that I'm going to find something worthwhile in it. That will be enough to push my body forward and allow me to hear the thing unspool itself, run out to the end.

// **21** //

I have been listening while running to the audio of a performance by Curtis Mayfield on German TV in 1972 for the show *Beat-Club*. There's a full program—twenty-five minutes or so—and rehearsal footage of about the same length, with fabulous camerawork and sound. It is the same band that made the record *Curtis/Live!*, and includes the great drummer Tyrone McCullen, who seems to have no other credits besides playing on a few Curtis Mayfield records. What happened to him?

Curtis Mayfield wrote lyrics about race and class divisions with depth and conflicted emotions. He sings with the sensitivity of a narrator who keeps an open mind and would like to resolve the conflict in himself, and others, without raising his voice—even if he can't. In the *Beat-Club* performance he sings "Stare and Stare," a description from the point of view of a silent passenger on a city bus, taking it all in: the fear, the snobbishness, the isolation, the desire for trust. It's a bleak song, made worse by the mode of encountering described—*staring*—but it never simplifies or moralizes. It seems to me more like a song about listening than about looking.

Mayfield sings lightly and plays the guitar without a pick; sometimes he seems to express the musicality of one who listens even more than he plays. How rare he was—although, according to a biography written by his son, he abused various women in his life and demanded such a high level of control in his work that he alienated those closest to him.

Can you use people by listening to them? Certainly: that's the definition of surveillance, and sometimes the definition of journalism. But if we are tempted to ascribe an absolute value to listening, perhaps it would be useful to talk about listening *toward* or *into*, rather than listening *at*.

Exemplary versions of the listening-toward or listening-into position can be found in art, fiction, journalism, teaching, dance, religion, protesting, work, love; I suppose it can be found in any human process. These listening positions are often related to some kind of lack: a regret, a fear, an anxiety, a distance, or a desire. But the listeners are not all the same. One of the best I ever met, and I met him only briefly, was Freddy Cole, Nat King Cole's brother. I was twenty-nine, and he was sixty-five. (Later I found out we had the same birthday.) It was before one of his gigs; I had arrived at the club early and he pulled a seat up next to mine, out of what I understood to be friendliness more than professional obligation. Unpretentious, even-tempered, and crinkly-eyed, he could tell I was distracted, tired, and generally in a hurry. (My memory says he didn't know what I was doing there, or that I'd come to review his performance; I had to tell him that.) He was just passing the time. He asked patient questions, nodding and commenting, and diagnosed me correctly as being in the middle of my "grinding years." He countered with a short description of his own, but only for about fifteen seconds before a full stop; then the even temper and crinkly eyes returned. He remained present while attending to me.

At a far end of the listening spectrum might be Simone Weil, who believed that listening was a zero-sum game: if you attend to the other person, especially someone afflicted, you can't remain present; you must effectively disappear, and this kind of listening—the most humane kind—isn't easily done, because it shouldn't be easy. "To listen to someone is to put oneself in his place while he is speaking," she wrote.

> To put oneself in the place of someone whose soul is corroded by affliction, or in near danger of it, is to annihilate oneself. It is more difficult than suicide would be for a happy child. Therefore the afflicted are not listened to. . . . That is why there is no hope for the vagrant as he stands before the magistrate.

It is difficult to talk about power relationships in the abstract, without knowing what they are. Perhaps it's best to live according to a theory of listening that presumes we are generally equal and able to look one another in the eye; from there we can adjust accordingly. The political scientist Susan Bickford tried to find this position in her book *The Dissonance of Democracy: Listening, Conflict, and Citizenship*, about listening as a political act in civil society. "The openness involved in listening," she wrote,

> is . . . an active willingness to construct certain relations of attention, relations in which neither of us has meaning without the other. This kind of listening and speaking together engages both agency and situatedness: I cannot hear you except against the ground of who I am, and you are speaking, not in the abstract, but to me—[or] to who you think your listeners are.

But neither side is involved in ritual self-abasement. Rather, the situation is improvised cooperatively. "The riskiness of listening comes partly from the possibility that what we hear will require change from us," she wrote.

This reminds me, again, of the book I've been reading, *The Brothers Karamazov*. Reading it is a struggle. It seems minimally edited into a book from its serial-publication form. A scene of insane repetition, motormouth dialogue, and tortuous plotting will be followed by a scene of scrupulous moral clarity, in which I can identify various characters and lines of description as people and things I have seen and known in my own life.

The character preventing me from abandoning the book is Alyosha, the mystic, the quiet one, the emotional doormat, fixed in the listening position as a consequence of both his temperament and his religious training. James Agee, in a letter to Dwight Macdonald in 1936—one film critic writing to another—imagined a movie version of Alyosha as played by Fred Astaire. I can picture that: the luminous forehead, the seminarian look of concern. The scenes with Alyosha have dynamism, even as a matter of visual graphing on the page: the other person says something and it's fifteen lines long; Alyosha responds with half a line. The other person drones on for another fifteen and Alyosha responds in one or two. And so forth. Through Alyosha's standpoint, Dostoyevsky makes the reader listen too. And the book is best when the reader occupies that position.

In music, the ones who best demonstrate the listening position are often not the soloists or the stars. Often they live in the rhythm section, like Billy Higgins or Charlie Watts, or they play an instrument with a history of accompaniment, like the violist Kim Kashkashian. Or they are producers, or engineers, or conductors.

One of the most unusual and imaginative I've known was Butch Morris, who conducted original music on the spot out of what he heard from the improvisers in his ensemble, listening and shaping their sound into repeatable forms with hand and body gestures, all while eliciting more of it. His music might have been weird, but the centrality he gave listening wasn't. He just went to work with tools that most of us are born with. The listening position can be found in the work of the visual artist David Hammons, a friend of Morris's, who once said in an interview, "I don't know what my work is. I have to wait and hear that from someone." It can be found in fictional characters who are highly sensitive receivers of talk and other communication; in novels by Dostoyevsky, Marcel Proust, Ralph Ellison, Uwe Johnson, Rachel Cusk, Sigrid Nunez, and probably thousands more; in Zora Neale Hurston's anthropological and personal essays "The Characteristics of Negro Expression," "Shouting," and "How It Feels to Be Colored Me"; in the very few essays John Berger wrote that deal with music, including "Field" and "Some Notes on Song"; in the analysts and cops on the television series *In Treatment* and *The Bridge*; in certain judges on vocal-competition shows like *The Voice* or *American Idol*; in the audience shots of Umm Kulthum performances and *The T.A.M.I. Show*. But in television or film, generally one glimpses the listening position only briefly. Listening does not convey action or narrative. The camera cuts to the listener only as a rhythmic trick, to break up the monotony of showing the speaker or singer.

For a while last year I found myself running with a bonanza of the listening position, in the Detroit dance-music producer Theo Parrish's two-and-a-half-hour audio essay *We Are All Georgeous Monsterss*—a gatherum of spoken Black voices from commercial recordings, friends telling stories into his microphone, YouTube rips of the recorded James Baldwin–Nikki Giovanni colloquy on TV from 1971, sometimes arranged over and around the beats of his strange and defiant techno music, and sometimes just left alone: a sustained act of listening as much as an organization of sound. There is an aspect of attending to others, and even a protection of others, involved in listening. But those who are great at it are usually not self-aggrandizing about it, because the best listening begins by distrusting and going beyond what is visible, whereas self-aggrandizement is always visible. That summer, Parrish made *Georgeous Monsterss* public for streaming, without announcement or explanation. Then after a few months he removed it—poof!—as if to say: "If you really listened to it, now you can remember it."

// **22** //

I go on a long one to set a wide frame for the year ahead and to dedicate my attention to what is coming.

I take with me Theo Parrish's four-hour DJ set from last July 4, which he created remotely for Elsewhere, a club I like in Brooklyn, part of which I'd heard at home during its live broadcast while putting together a chest of drawers and making dinner. Lately I've been giving a monthly donation to the club, which I never enter, as it's temporarily closed. In return, I have the privilege, on cold mornings, of listening to club sets that weren't created in the club and weren't really meant to exist outside of its proper hot-evening chronological moment.

But I think I can run analogously to Theo Parrish's long DJ set, because part of taking in something like that under normal circumstances is psychological preconditioning: What will you need? How will you take care of yourself? What will you do for the rest of your day? How can you get on the same frequency with it and remain that way?

The light and air are like ginger, clarifying and real—forty-five degrees or so, sunny most of the time—and the set begins Parrish's "ugly edits" of some James Brown cuts. (Parrish makes what he calls "ugly edits" from vinyl sources, looping a short section of a song into such layered, repetitive, lengthy density that the tiny portion assumes grand significance.) He focuses his will to repeat on the sequences that are most full of Brown's chatter and encouragement, making repetitions out of repetitions, ending with "Doing It to Death," in which Parrish loops Brown's abiding chants until their ritual aspect takes over.

> I feel so down, I need to get down, / in order for me to get down I gotta / get in D. / . . . Need to get in D. / Dog the D, down D. / Funky D, stankin' D. / Down D!

Then the change down to the D chord arrives, followed by Brown's catapulting laugh, and the band joining the chant on the chorus: "We gotta have a funky good time," Brown shouts to Fred Wesley, the band's trombonist.

"I didn't know you were singing, Fred!"

"I'm moaning."

"Don't moan so much, brother. Don't moan so *much*!"

The last *I* in the word "higher," normally held for two bars, gets stretched and looped by Parrish for about seventy seconds, nearly disintegrating into digital noise, and in each loop you can hear the LP's distortions as it wavers out of tune, as if the record were going to drive off the road. We're not quite half an hour into Parrish's set. After James Brown, it's Ray de la Paz singing with Ray Barretto, Kai Alcé's remix of Gregory Porter singing about Harlem, and some of Parrish's own music, including with the singer Maurissa Rose, unnerving and ghostly, sketchy and off-center, also persevering, also warm: How does he do that? What a complicated emotion, if it is an emotion. It doesn't need to be.

This is the season to do things differently and capaciously, to make the cleaning happen continuously as I go, to consider the knuckleball, to think about what all the givens are doing. Parrish moves through long passages of great joy, but always with some turbulence: awkwardness, roughness, bumpiness, fragmented phrase repetition. If you are willing to stay with him, he will make you hear slightly differently.

I run some usual routes in the reverse direction, up hills and down hills. I want to find high altitudes and also the river level, and I want to see my ten-mile radius for what it is: leafy, quiet neighborhoods and projects; one-way streets where I can run the wrong way without encountering a single car, and market boulevards. In parts of southwest Yonkers the gritty blocks are sumptuous, with bright colors and movement and stirring smells of tortillas, cigarette smoke, and machine parts, while the upscale blocks are drab and dowdy and empty.

I run past the house where Gene Krupa retreated after he served jail time for marijuana put in his coat pocket by his valet; up toward the blocks where DMX and Ella Fitzgerald spent their youths; then down toward the river, past the scene of an accident I read about in the local paper: two days before Christmas, a driver fleeing the police sped through a light and cleaved a car in half. Everyone died. The car carried four teenagers who'd graduated from high school that spring. I stopped by a makeshift memorial—candles, sneakers, flowers—to read some letters to one of the young men from his true loves—family or romantic or platonic, what does it matter? Such grief. Meanwhile, over Parrish's spartan garage-programming of bongo sounds, shakers, and clicks, Maurissa Rose sings: "And for the way you gave sacrificially—brother, this is for you."

The sky is turning gray, but the gray doesn't have the usual emotional correlative. Moving, and the perspective it affords, has shaken it loose.

// 23 //

A study published in 2017 by some kinesiologists from California used a particular methodology to assess ten runners' thoughts in real time: "Through years of research testing and exploration," the authors of the study wrote, "researchers have concluded that when individuals are asked to simply verbalize what is going through their heads without trying to explain or describe it, they are able to accurately capture thought processes without affecting performance." The participants had in the past completed at least a half-marathon, and were training for another. They all ran at least twenty miles a week, or at least three times a week: not so very much, when you get right down to it; not Murakami levels. Their experience with running varied between three and thirty years: at one end, that's not very long. What did they think about?

Forty percent of the marathoners' thoughts were sorted into the category of "pace and distance" ("Downhill, don't kill yourself, just cruise"); 32 percent into "pain and discomfort" ("Ugh, I feel like shit. Why did my period have to come now?"); 28 percent into thoughts about environmental matters of weather or wildlife or traffic ("These trees are so cool in the wind," or "Is that a rabbit at the end [of the] road? Oh yeah, how cute").

My marathoner friends describe some of their thoughts similarly. But they also think, they tell me, of obligations and regrets, things their brain has told them to remember: laundry, or whether they spoke out of turn the day before. When the running gets good, they might think about various kinds of gratitude, or about fullness or emptiness. As one friend put it, when she realizes she hears no sound from her sneakers, she knows her stride has improved. When the running is really good, it seems, something like a void may be possible, or at least a state of mind that has no compulsion to generate anything special, anything in particular.

How about positive depictions of thinking while running? I'll take them from anywhere. I'll take them from a fictional character.

I'll take Smith, the fictional young runner in Alan Sillitoe's 1959 short story "The Loneliness of the Long-Distance Runner." Smith is stuck in a Borstal, a detention center for youth offenders. He runs around the property every day to keep sane, while figuring out how to deny the Borstal director (the "governor") the pleasure of paternalistic gloating over rehabilitating a scruff and, perhaps, denying him the spoils of a bet on Smith to win first in the Borstal Blue Ribbon Prize Cup for Long Distance Cross Country Running (All England).

Smith says:

> This long-distance running lark is the best of all, because it makes me think so good that I learn things even better than when I'm on my bed at night. . . .
>
> At the moment it's dead blokes like [the governor] who have the whip-hand over blokes like me, and I'm almost dead sure it'll always be like that, but even so, by Christ, I'd rather be like I am—always on the run and breaking into

shops for a packet of fags and a jar of jam—than have the whip-hand over somebody else and be dead from the toe nails up. Maybe as soon as you get the whip-hand over somebody you do go dead. By God, to say that last sentence has needed a few hundred miles of long-distance running. . . .

Because you see I never race at all; I just run, and somehow I know that if I forget I'm racing and only jog-trot along until I don't know I'm running I always win the race. For when my eyes recognize that I'm getting near the end of the course—by seeing a stile or cottage corner—I put on a spurt, and such a fast big spurt it is because I feel that up till then I haven't been running and that I've used up no energy at all. And I've been able to do this because I've been thinking; and I wonder if I'm the only one in the running business with this system of forgetting that I'm running because I'm too busy thinking; and I wonder if any of the other lads are on to the same lark, though I know for a fact that they aren't.

I am not at all sure that Sillitoe ran. Here is how he describes the sound of running:

Trot-trot-trot. Puff-puff-puff. Slap-slap-slap go my feet on the hard soil. Swish-swish-swish as my arms and side catch the bare branches of a bush.

I know those sounds: the puff and the slap are the sounds of the first month, maybe the first hundred miles, maybe the first fifty, before you stop caring about where your body ends and where the air begins, before you stop coming down so heavily on your feet, because in a sense the feet aren't there, you have to remind yourself that you even have feet, before you realize that at the moment of beginning to run your matter changes. Later:

Flip-flap, flip-flap, jog-trot, jog-trot, crunchslap-crunchslap . . .

It's true what he says about feeling that you're not racing, just running—and about the sensation of using up no energy at all. But when you are free of the race, or free of any sense that running might be a chore or necessity, those wet, heavy sounds (flip, flap, slap, puff) recede. Those are the sounds of resistance.

If Sillitoe didn't run, perhaps he wished he could, while suffering from tuberculosis after serving in the Royal Air Force. Or perhaps he just found running a simple and handy metaphor, and one needn't take it literally. (Smith is a "runner" in the sense that he thieves and flees the scene of the crime, and in the sense that he will always be on the wrong end of authorities, and in the sense that he is a fictional male rebel-hero of the 1950s who goes it alone.)

But, yes, when you run, you are mostly alone, even if you have running friends; and the truthful motion engages thought that can lift you out of your limitations; and the comfortable tunnel of thought that opens itself to a runner can make the body disappear. It's the body that disappears, not the thinking.

But if Sillitoe got the sound of running wrong, what does it sound like?

// 24 //

Feet	Thought	Sound
Bom-bip, bom-bip, splash, skedge-skedge, skedge-skedge, skedge-skedge, skedge-skedge,	("The world is more fragile now." Schomburg Center. Students, enthusi-asm, one on one, soli-tude, free will, nobody cares whether you come or go, the good citizen, Portuguese, "ee, down-down-da-dey, down-down-da-dey; ee . . ." Paula Rego, Naná Vasconcelos, LSD, naked on Canal Street, rhythm for melody, keeping some-thing for yourself, the lower depths, I'm going away for a while, "free bird," meetings, consensus, a lot to an-swer for, stamp on the envelope, perhaps they were avoiding it. Car,	Ssssssss

Tuweeeeee, tuwee-tuwee-tu-tu-tu-tuwee-tu-tu-tuweee

(Irradiating pain in foot, experienced almost as a sound)

Não mas tome cuidado

AaaaaaAAAA! AAAAA! What, what, what, what, what?

KsssssssSSSSSSsssssss

There's gotta be a way around it |

skedge-skedge, skedge-skedge, skedge-skedge, skedge-skedge, skedge-skedge, skedge-skedge, bom-bip, bom-bip, bom-bip, bom-bip, bom-bip, bom-bip, bom-bip, bom-bip, bom-bip, bom-bip, bom-bip, bom-bip, bom-bip, bom-bip, bom-bip, bom-bom, bom-bom, bom-bom, bom-bom, bom-bom, bom-bom, bom-bom, bom-bom.	A train, dusk at 8:30, smoke, noise, currents on currents, micro-climate, the hard-ness or softness of the internal organs, a straight answer, hold-ing two opposing ideas at the same time. Committee hearings, now or later, happen-stance, the mass emo-tion in real time.)	KsssssCraaaAAAAAAA Tongtongtongtong tongtongtongtong tongtongtongtong tongtongtongtong tongtong I thought you knew where we were!

// 25 //

The new sound in my running is a pain in my right foot like gong-swells along muscle and bone. Occasionally the foot protests being used, and occasionally it couldn't care less. The foot doesn't much like walking at all. Running hurts it a lot, but not quite enough to stop running on it. The foot complains in the first twenty minutes, acquiesces for a long stretch, then complains again at the end. This kind of pain has come and gone over the last five years. I'll book a new visit to the podiatrist, who will probably tell me what he told me last time: Arthritis is common. My expensive inserts will keep doing what they can.

Six months ago, my older brother and I moved my father into assisted living, about five hours from New York City. During the assisted-living period, we did much that required attention and persistence: talking to doctors; dividing our father's things into needed and not-needed, given his latest cognitive state; and, for me, long-haul driving. He seemed abstracted in the presence of all machines and the question of how to turn music on or off, but he liked a playlist I made for him that included a lot of music performed alone or with only one other person: Eric Dolphy playing "God Bless the Child," Martha Argerich playing Chopin, Jenny Lin playing Frederic Mompou, Sylvia Rexach singing her songs with the guitarist Tuti Umpierre, Caetano Veloso singing his songs with the clarinetist Ivan Sacerdote, Kashkashian playing Bach, Ólafsson playing Debussy.

He took great pleasure in a book of Murakami short stories during this period, reading and rereading it and having it read to him, particularly a hallucinatory story called "Cream," in which the narrator receives a strange invitation from an old, distant acquaintance to attend a piano recital on top of a mountain. So on the appointed day and time, the narrator takes a bus up the mountain and walks to the recital spot, but the building where the recital is to take place is abandoned, and has been padlocked. He's the only person in sight. Bewildered, he begins walking back down the mountain, stopping at a park that had escaped his notice on the way up, and starts hyperventilating, worrying he's been pranked. When he comes to, an old man has appeared beside him. The old man starts talking about "a circle that has several centers and no circumference," to the narrator's great confusion.

The old man allows that it is very difficult to imagine this circle, but when you do, you've achieved the "crème de la crème," the "most important essence of life." My father liked the idea of the cream of one's life; his partner, after reading him the story, had the inspired idea to help him draw up a list of things in his life that he felt amounted to the cream of it.

I wondered, then and now, whether this circle might not represent a properly complex experience of living or, equally, a properly complex experience of listening: you're in a life, or you're in a song, and by default you feel you're at its center, but the seeming position of the center keeps changing with you, according to time and circumstances, and if there's a "circumference"—or a beginning and an end, perhaps—you can't easily perceive it.

Also, for what it's worth, a song can have more than one key center, and most thoughts, sensations, and emotions are hybrid: they have more than one aspect.

After three months in the facility, my father died. The cause of death was "inanition," a word I hadn't heard or read before. It means emptiness. He did it: he acquired a void, like Murakami, like the *komuso*. Shortly after my father's death, I finally got COVID-19. Less than a month later I got something else that felt close to COVID but wasn't, and then my wife got COVID too. I never took a break from teaching, and teaching has been hard lately. Well, it was hard around the time of his death: I was limp and emotional whether I'd slept or not; I got unnerved and would lose track of what I was saying. But I mean that teaching during this point in the history of the world has been a bit hard. The weird privations have led to something that reads on student faces like mute loneliness. We murmur, "At least we're not ——" (dying of a virus, running from a wildfire, hiding in a basement in Ukraine, experiencing severe thirst). But we are frequently another ——.

There is some physical exhaustion involved in open or sublimated grief. I can remember experiencing it after my mother died. I don't have it quite as badly this time, but I understand that the extra difficulty I have in getting going in the morning might have to do with the morbid shadow. I do also feel as if I might have temporarily lost something over the period of time when I was too sick to run: some underlying free energy. I have wondered whether this is called falling out of shape (though it's not as if I truly stopped doing things!), or lack of will, or whether the last six months just made me older by a provable notch, as one always imagines the next birthday will do. But I am also bored by the question. How can anyone know what the problem is? And what good would it do? A runner just keeps going.

o

I find I can get excited about listening to music that corresponds with the struggle I've been experiencing: music that perhaps only reluctantly lends itself to forward motion, or that achieves its ends with obvious effort, maybe even pain. Naturally, it must be animated from within somehow: music that has unquantifiable energy in it somewhere. If I can come to feel in tune with the struggle, rather than pushing against it, I'll be better off.

I listen to a record of Iannis Xenakis's percussion music played by Alexandros Giovanos and run on the old railroad path heading north on a stirring spring morning, something like sixty degrees, cool enough for my sweat to grow cold.

Xenakis's "Rebonds" is written for pitched and spirit-filled drums: bongos, tumbadora, tom-toms, and bass drum. Giovanos whacks the bongos and tumbadora, sometimes extremely hard, with sticks; it doesn't produce the hand drum sound one's used to hearing from them. The patterns flow in and out of phase, counter to a normal, repeated running gait; if you have ever run upstairs, stopping briefly on a step to switch your leading foot, thereby breaking the smooth rhythm you've created, you can imagine the way this piece keeps splintering its own forward motion.

Then "Kassandra," for percussion: this is what I've been looking for! My body may be disobeying me, but my instincts seem to be working.

"Kassandra" is not easy to listen to, and not easy to enact. It's a duet for drums of the same general type as in "Rebonds," with a male baritone singing in a falsetto and playing a twenty-string psaltery, the ancient Greek zither-like instrument. Perhaps because of the implications of Xenakis's graphic score, or perhaps because the singer is embodying a Trojan woman forcibly taken to Greece, and (as punishment for refusing Apollo's sexual desire) stripped of an intelligible voice whenever she must tell the truth, the baritone—Martin Gerke, in the version I am listening to—defines the feeling I am looking for: a desire that has lost its shape but needs to keep expressing.

A few minutes into "Kassandra," as I run I am uncomfortable. The music is hard to connect with body motion. I feel as if I am testing my thesis that I can listen to anything while running: perhaps not this. But a few minutes in I become very happy, without even experiencing the shift, and this may be because my pain is beginning to recede, or I am thinking less about it. I am thinking about the implications of the music as well as its outer aspects. (There is not an aural equivalent to the word "aspect.") I am beginning to feel excited and to fall in line.

Then a woman runs down the straight path in my direction, fast: a young woman I noticed yesterday on a quiet block close to my building, running sprints back and forth. She's looking ahead with a neutral expression, wearing glasses and lifting her knees high, cutting a thin line straight through the atmosphere. She proceeds in a far less dramatic way than the music. She does not represent the temper of the music I have in my ears, but rather its level of commitment. At this point, I am released; I seem to have left the pain behind. I think about it and consider it not there. The thesis remains intact. Beats per minute has no relation to this music whatsoever, nor does repetition, nor does discernible heroism or familiarity or the notion of a good mood. But the music is moving forward and it is committed. Its reserves of will are enormous. What makes the environment of the music? Anger, dread, certainty. I can run through that.

Finally, "Psappha," thirteen minutes long, again for solo percussion. It keeps steady patterns, then breaks them; it allows big open pockets of silence, but it is altogether more integrated and self-confident than "Rebonds." It sounds like the finished work for which "Rebonds" might have been a trial or sketch. I am enjoying it so much as I move that I listen to the entire track twice.

// 26 //

The other night I sat in a basement and heard the pianist David Virelles, in a trio with the bassist Ben Street and the drummer Eric McPherson, play a version of Charlie Parker's "Ornithology." That song is seventy-six years old, and it embodies a style, bebop, that has passed through the thrill of its gestation and arrival into waves of competitive homage, deconstructed reference, academic study, and whatever comes after that. It's so tangible, bebop is, with lots of harmonic and rhythmic trademarks, but it became clichéd within ten years of its beginning, or maybe even five. Played these days, it rarely sounds good—if you hear it, which you mostly won't, outside of classrooms.

But these three make bebop sound good. They make it pulsate, so the strong and counterintuitive grace of its origin flushes to the surface. They make it come alive, and when something is truly alive, it never becomes a sign or a symbol or an attribute of something else. It is too busy escaping you. This is exactly what the best part of running is like, I thought, while squished into a banquette. Jazz clubs as we know them today were formed around bebop, a music that theoretically wants you to move, because of its roots in dance music and its surface-level energy, but that in practice holds you rooted to the spot with the tension of its rushed beats and its abundance of chords.

So I think of that music today, looking for a prod. Sixty-five degrees this morning, and a bit of humidity before a rainstorm. I am feeling healthy and well rested, ready to go back to one of my old, longer routes, and here are Charlie Parker's complete recordings on Savoy and Dial, three hours long. No foot pain at the beginning of my run, until it appears about five minutes in. Well then, I'll go with this music's optimism, its practiced confidence, its vitality, and its quantity. There is a lot of it, in short doses. "Red Cross," "Warming Up a Riff," "Billie's Bounce," "Now's the Time," "Thriving on a Riff," "Meandering." . . . These songs play with one's focus: the details within a single bar of music can rearrange you for minutes afterward, but by that time you'll be on the next track, so at some point you are nearly forced to start letting it all wash over you.

This music accompanies me up one of the steepest hills in my area, three hundred feet above sea level, according to a topographical map of Yonkers, one of those runs that goes through varying degrees of steepness until I'm walking with jumps—that's essentially what I'm doing—and then a landing appears, a flat stretch, and then another rise comes after that. This is the sort of running that requires one to settle one's mind and give in. No opinions about anything are formed during these periods. No questions are moved toward resolution. I'm merely going dumb, but I can use that in the service of awe. Parker's playing is so fluid and fresh, it's as if he can shoot a scattergun into the next measure and find ways to connect his ten new widely spaced targets with melodic improvisation.

After I go down the hill, running through blocks of Mexican cafés and tire and auto-glass shops, a track comes on with a faltering beginning. I don't register the tune from its introduction, but it turns out to be "Lover Man," the infamous recording he made while experiencing heroin-withdrawal spasms, released against his wishes by Ross Russell, the head of Dial Records. Haven't heard it for a long time. The record has been so often analyzed as a deterministic event in the narrative of Parker's life that it's good to come upon it by surprise. I can hear from the beginning that something's wrong with him, but what he's able to do in the middle of the tune strikes me as at least honorable; he delivers a Charlie Parker performance. Perhaps that's the problem: this performance is more like a promissory note.

As I listen I realize it took me a long time to understand this frailty. Nearly as soon as I started learning about jazz, I heard about the "Lover Man" session, and I didn't get it: What's so bad about this? Why the controversy, back then, over the record being released? Anyone playing any music that is not of the academy, of an institution, is likely to be impaired in some way because of protocols around that music and liabilities of its culture: inadequate preparation, inadequate health care, drugs, alcohol, lack of sleep. . . . People falter in a song and then often recover somewhat, as Charlie Parker is clearly doing here. I do hear some disarray, but I mostly hear someone rising to the occasion.

Or perhaps the problem is that his gift was beyond understanding, and hearing him sputter is too easily understood as a narrative of suffering and disarray, rendering the music inert. So Russell's betrayal wasn't so much in releasing to the world a version of Parker when he was not at his best, but in restricting him to the holding pen of a story: a story about a defeated person.

I suddenly feel my foot again. Well, I can pretend it's not

there. The album gets into the 1947 session with the singer Earl Coleman, the ballads "This Is Always" and "Dark Shadows," and the buoyancy has gone out of this run a little bit. It's been an hour and a quarter. I am nearly home when the pain is too great and I come to a stop; as I do, the ache seems to billow outward.

// 27 //

A friend texts me *Information*, a record from a few years ago by Galcher Lustwerk, the house producer from Brooklyn, and I'm off. The heat has become serious during these few weeks—even at 8 a.m. it's eighty-five degrees with 60 percent humidity—so level running is the way to go, nothing too dramatic. Keep the overhead low. Let the music tell me what it has to tell me, and run in response.

Running is dailiness, and one can choose to give the phrase "daily practice" a ring of holiness or of work ethic. It sounds like meditation, it sounds like taking inventory, it sounds like a regimen to protect the body. But what if daily practice is just doing something for no immediate result, just for the feeling, like making marks on paper to see how they look? When I meet my running with respect but no ambition, I can feel it best: bipedal constancy, the infinite present, the loosening of time.

Galcher Lustwerk's quiet dance tracks hold themselves elegantly. He speaks parlando phrases over the music, which generally contains three drumlike elements, whether digital or material—hi-hat, snare drum, and kick drum—and background synthesizer chordal washes. The tracks light up well enough with pure digital rhythm, but when he adds the sound of a real hi-hat, played with a real hand, the beats repeating unostentatiously in a medium tempo, the record becomes something else again. Imagine his angle of intent turned just a little bit and you could be listening to music specifically for "relaxing," or for spending money, or for romance. But the difference is in his spin on the beat, both within the individual bar and on a macro level. He's not leading you toward much. He's simply focusing on the now. It sounds as if the microphone and whatever minimal drum kit are close but not *very* close: about the distance between a drummer's ears and his hands. So you're not at audience distance from the music, nor are you artificially close to it, closer than a listener might reasonably be. Your relationship to the music is the maker's relationship to the music, and the maker, for lack of a better word, sounds like he's practicing. I am running at Galcher Lustwerk mid-tempo, but more important, I am running alongside his practicing.

Practicing for what? Maybe to become a better drummer, or maybe as a matter of routine maintenance—sure, if you want. But when I hear the record, I retain the image of a woodworker alone in his shop, working on his organic material with repeated small motions, not expecting to get anywhere fast. Is he building something? Well, yes, the woodworker is building something, maybe a table, and Galcher Lustwerk is building a track; anyone who sets up a shop or puts out records has learned to finish things. The track or the table is simply the outcome, not a method or the reason it was made. The reason this music doesn't sound like it's for spending money, relaxing, or for romance, is because he appears to be practicing. What if he's not practicing for anything? Same with running: What if it's not practice for anything?

Before I left the house this morning, I read in the newspaper the latest of the frequent articles about Denmark being the happiest country in the world. Newspaper editors presume that we all want to know how they do it. The gist of the piece was that the Danes' happiness comes down to a basic level of trust—in family, friends, communal values, and even elected leaders—and regularly doing things with friends that don't cost money, such as walking in nature. I haven't been to Denmark, but as I run today, listening to the metal of Galcher Lustwerk's hi-hat and his respect for practice, I wave to my daily running friends, and consider that I go to Denmark every time I put on my shoes and start my headlong motion. Meanwhile, Galcher Lustwerk's been singing something in an understated mumble, something like munna-munna-munna-affa-kah. A minute after my thought about Denmark, I realize what he's been repeating: "I feel like I'm in Africa / I ain't never been to Africa."

// 28 //

Gray day outside; it was raining when I arose, but it stopped, and it looked to be gray but clear for several hours. Making my way out the door, I ran into a neighbor—a nice man—with his kid. "You going to run in *this*?" he asked, looking through the front doorway. I asked him if it was actually raining. He looked outside again. "No . . ." It just seemed like the sort of day for staying in.

I was distracted, having already started on my track: Bach's Concerto for Two Violins, with Rachel Podger as the lead violinist. The answer is that circumstances look ideal out there— the kind that require a little adjustment, a change of perspective before you realize that you're in for something very rich, something that's not easy to grasp all at once, something that reveals itself to you slowly but retains a mysterious coherence. A day for the heads, not the casual fans.

Southwest Yonkers: Saturday-morning laundry smells suggest and then assert themselves. I am running on a narrow sidewalk by apartment buildings and small houses, and the kitchens or basements or wherever the washers are can't be more than fifty feet from me. Auto-grease smells from the Don-Glo service center, where cars are up on risers, getting inspected. Steam-chemical smells from the dry cleaner. The faintest whiff of mildew from the roadside private-garage fronts. Microclimates of cannabis smoke: Where is it coming from? I don't see anyone.

The pieces on this Podger record, *Bach: Double & Triple Concertos*, featuring two or three instruments—two or three violins, or violin and oboe, or violin, flute, and harpsichord—motor along seriously, booming, almost thumping. It's Podger's group, Brecon Baroque. The harpsichordist, Marcin Świątkiewicz, hits hard in the allegro movements, emphasizing the short double time rips, letting you feel the instrument as if it were drums. That's just it: the timbre of his playing and the subdivided bits where he speeds up and slows down remind me of English drum-and-bass music from the '90s; even better than that, he introduces uncertainty into the tempos, so the whole ensemble has to tie itself to his agogic drift.

Bach's music reveals itself now slowly but completely. The sureness of his patterns, rhythmically and harmonically, allows you to sense something coming slightly before it does. Then it happens, the melodic run or key change, and it stays with you, in your ears and in your body, for some time afterward. He's building a fresh and credible city for you, essentially, as you walk through it; he does the work just before you get there. It is not a simple city. It's dense with protocols: all those little trills for the grace of it, like detergent perfume, tell you that. The moods can shift severely, are foreboding. I see two men up ahead on a narrow park trail, walking slowly in the center of the path: Who are they? Beyond them, barely visible, are two red vehicle lights. Is something wrong? Nothing to do but to approach, to move through it, to move on to the next leg.

It rains quite seriously toward the end of what's become a ninety-minute run. I don't mind, because I'm deep in the lesson. The runners and walkers I pass in the rain, smiling, satisfied within themselves, don't mind either.

// 29 //

A runner is a private self in public. Fred Astaire sings with the voice of a small private soul, a person talking to himself or rehearsing an exchange that has yet to happen. Maybe he's getting ready to go out, or to enter a party—two of his best-known songs, both written by Irving Berlin, describe this: a guy dressing up for the evening in "Top Hat, White Tie and Tails"; a guy marveling at the passaggio outside the club in "Puttin' On the Ritz." You feel the narrator's awareness of his heart rate, his breathing. When you close up your ears and talk softly, so your private self fills your head: that's how he sounds. He's good in earphones. What's more, he allows the private self to be graceful.

On the album *The Astaire Story*, from 1952, he sings with a jazz quintet led by Oscar Peterson—something different for Astaire, who was used to singing with Hollywood and Broadway arrangements. Everything has been arranged with him at the center: the record's got his name on it, the engineer has pushed his voice high in the mix, and Astaire sometimes drops in for spoken introductions, indicating how the songs have fit into his working life. Conceived by the jazz producer Norman Granz, who had to talk Astaire into making it, the album is built entirely of songs that Astaire first made known through his performances in movies and onstage; in some cases, they were songs written expressly for him to sing. But Astaire sounds diffident.

Or perhaps publicly confident and privately diffident—in any case, a bit unreachable; he's saving something for himself. The introductions sound like interior monologues. You imagine he suspects this exercise is too much; you keep expecting him to say, "Oh, never mind."

> This one my little sister Adele and I did in *The Band Wagon* at the New Amsterdam theater in New York—back in, uh, let me see, nineteen twentyyyy . . . nine, I think. Yah. Well, anyway, uh, it was one of our biggest shows. *Terrific* cast: Frank Morgan, Helen Broderick, Tilly Losch, and . . . oh . . . lots of . . . wonderful people . . .

The width of his signal seems scaled to a cabaret-sized room, maybe a small basement club, but more precisely one in which he is somehow there and not there beside the band. He might even be in the audience, singing along so that only he can hear his own voice.

Those introductions are sometimes strangely apologetic. Before "Not My Girl," a song he cowrote, he offers: "I'll start off by playing the first chorus in the same style as I used to do it then; Oscar rescues me and takes it from there." And so he begins the tune at the piano himself, but he has *announced* that he will do this (how clinical to do that on a studio record), even draws attention to his inadequacy, though he is really only a bit stiff and antiquated, not a terrible player at all.

Astaire had been an entertainer since the age of six, and so a listener should be under no illusion that the apologetic manner is "real"; we might consider that the "real" is very hard to find here, possibly even for him. Still, performance or not, he makes you aware that he is the oldest man in the room; he makes you aware that he is a man from a time and context that have ended. The only way he can get through this with self-respect is by surprising you, giving you something you didn't know you wanted, or making you understand that the present flows from the past.

The idea keeps striking me, as I run through carpets of wet leaves, that he is singing along with these songs as much as singing them. It seems an unprofessional or paraprofessional act. He spoke self-effacingly about his singing, and he was right to. His tone is thin and his pronunciation square, and his intonation, though excellent for a non-singer, falls slightly off sometimes. Perhaps he didn't take audio recording very seriously. Toward the end of Oscar Peterson's introductory chorus on "Dancing in the Dark," you hear Astaire breathe in through his nose rather loudly, as if he doesn't know—or doesn't particularly care—that we're going to hear that. Often he mutters "Unh" or "Yeah!" or finishes a word with a sharp exhalation of breath, as if he doesn't know we're going to hear that either. He laughs just a little, a chuckle in his nose or throat, tiny horselike snorts. "You were going on your way, / now you've got to remain," he sings on "Isn't This a Lovely Day," and Charlie Shavers follows with a little muted-trumpet obbligato; Astaire, noticing, breathes "*Hmm.*" In "I've Got My Eyes on You" he pronounces the word "in-ci-dent-al-lee" like someone who likes memorizing verb declensions: an exact pronunciation, not hip at all. In only a few places on the record does he sound like an ace at making records. One is on "Night and Day"—the whole tune—during which, possibly, he is remembering how virtuosic he had been during the danced and filmed version of that song. Another is at the last moment of "Nice Work If You Can Get It," when he praises the band by purring, "Nice work."

So Astaire might not be excelling, at least in terms of the standards of records in 1952. He might not have cared to. He might have been all right with it. "The whole business," decided Douglas Watt in his *New Yorker* review of the album, "should have had the bright surface excitement of a Broadway pit band, instead of the languid air of an after-hours jam session by tired musicians in somebody's back room."

But if Astaire is not a good singer, he is also a great one. *The Astaire Story* is enormously long: originally released as a four-record box set, it presents two and a half hours of singing along and breathing along. The idea that Astaire might approach the songs—some of them "standards" written for him, but for his body first and his voice second—by stepping into them lightly, taking them for a ride in amateur bliss without stamping into them his proof of ownership, without gripping them as Oscar Peterson does: what a buoying way to make music. Easy come, easy go. Let the rain pitter-patter, but it really doesn't matter. The songs will last; we won't.

Astaire versus the songbook, alongside me and the atmosphere. Look at this day: medium cold and medium wet, slate-gray skies and dying leaves colored from yellow to almost black, a straight zip of paved path pointed all the way to Albany. It's ridiculous how inviting it feels. I can't grip this, I can't own it; best I can do is sing along to it. This means voluntarily breaking the spell and liking it: slowing down, looking around, regularly noticing my own breathing rhythm, even walking for a while if I feel like it.

Singing along in a running sense also might mean that I can be rhythmically out of sync with the environment; it, too, doesn't matter. Astaire does something like this during "(Ad Lib) Slow

Dances," in which Peterson and the rhythm section—Ray Brown, Alvin Stoller, Barney Kessel—stroll on the blues, and Astaire taps almost an entire beat too fast. He hasn't called a tempo; he's just getting in and messing around, and the band knows better than to adjust to him. The result is not an example of perfect rhythmic linkage, but happiness that can be generated by discrepancies. There it is: the difference between me and this path and its atmosphere—the degree to which I am just a visitor to it, an admirer, a not particularly good runner in it—may be worth preserving as its own virtue.

To hear this record is to be satisfied that one has a private self. Not a dramatized, heroic private self—as music is so good at conveying—but a slightly ordinary one. The idea of this private self confronts the listener and becomes a companion. Still, Astaire is willing to hang with this, to participate in an extremely long experiment, even one that seems slightly against his instincts or his wishes. He respects the musicians and, possibly, they respect him. Oscar Peterson, we are told in a biography by Gene Lees, wore a gold bracelet given to him after the sessions by Astaire—engraved "With Thanks, Fred A."—at all times except while fishing. (The musicians also complement his shortcomings: the tenor saxophonist Flip Phillips seems to know he should play low-end ballad tones to make up for the lack of a low end in Astaire's voice.) Astaire is a worker in this endeavor, and he will be present within it, and it will be great, because in addition to the studious diction and the thin voice, he is Fred Astaire.

I have run short and long with this record, on straight, flat lines and up terrible hills, probably on every day of the week, in both the city and the country. I find that to the extent that running is hard work, the performance honors hard work; and to the extent that running is play, the performance honors play. It represents a strange and contradictory mixture of unquestioning, nearly self-erasing commitment and an awareness that living is essentially a matter of lightness, of being next to the thing rather than on it, of commenting and annotating and chiming in from the side.

// 30 //

I bought a new phone and learned that it doesn't log any information about how many miles you've run with it (and all other information about "health"), unless you set up that app by feeding it information about yourself. If you don't, it won't tell you how far you've gone. Good: the phone is forbearing. Can I keep it that way—can I hold it off? I really don't want to know how far I've gone. If the phone makes the information available to me, I may look at it, and then it's over: running becomes data again.

Narratives suggest a range of forms, of course, sometimes a range of arcs, and often a magnetized "ending place"—at least a theoretical one, as distinct from the actual ending of any text or story—so that the teller does not become lost. These elements, which in many ways have been previously determined and refined through a culture and a people, protect the teller and also the reader or listener. A narrative allows a reader to follow more securely (I am thinking of the phrase "secure data"), and also allows them a sturdy form, so the narrative can be retold.

The retelling of narrative can preserve a culture and a system of values, even a sensibility, even to some degree the spirit of a people, and this preservation has importance: it can counteract all the titled and monopolizing forces in the world, the culture and values of the people who own the most things. And narrative can also be creatively disobeyed and upended, drawn out or condensed—it's all in how you do it, as long as you agree that narrative is important enough to convolute.

Narrative keeps promising, and sometimes threatening, to do more. It creates an amiable kind of consistency, then a standard, then suddenly a system. I'm curious about something I heard Hans Magnus Enzensberger say in a 1981 lecture I listened to recently: "Consistency will turn any good cause into a bad one." If you follow a set of values to its logical conclusion, he suggests, you end up ruining the system you're participating in.

> Act out the fundamental tenets of capitalism to their ultimate consequences, and you will end up with civil war and a fascist dictatorship. Attack the social system you live in by any means at your disposal, and you have terrorism; defend it by any means, and you have a Gestapo running the place. Be a rigorous ecologist and defend nature against man with no holds barred, and you will end up leading a Stone Age existence. Build communism, be uncompromising about it, and your militancy will take you straight into what is rightly known as the socialist camp. Pursue economic growth at any price and you will destroy the biosphere. Join the arms race, be consistent about it, and you will blow yourself to pieces. Et cetera.

He is engaging in his own kind of narrative here, following his own idea to a logical conclusion, but even someone who is not Enzensberger might allow that the essence of narrative is different from the essence of moment-to-moment experience; and in the moment-to-moment experience, the line or arc of narrative is hard, or sometimes impossible, to discern.

Hard to live without principles! I wouldn't want to do it; I can't defend such a way of living. But I don't think I'm suggesting it, either. Each run has a beginning and an end. The beginning and the end are graceful moments, moments of distinction, strong gestures. I would like to feel them as deeply as I can. I'd like to understand them from what Enzensberger might call a position of "inconsistency"—somewhere in the middle, a position from which they are neither nonsense nor settled theory, from which they can't be completely understood, yet have meaning. Religion might be that position, loath as I am to admit it.

Or being halfway through life might be that position. I have accomplished enough (as nearly everyone does in one way or another) that I can start to do the obvious next step, which is notdoing. By which I mean—I have to mean—forbearance rather than rejection, or letting things suggest their own correct arrangement, a kind of Ouija sifting rather than fighting toward a desired finish. The fight for a desired finish can come later and probably will, as I have learned from (another accomplishment) watching two parents die. That's it: pick up the principles of the fight later, when they have a shorter period in which to be enacted. I will no longer be able to run then.

So I am trying to run according to an idea of an amenable inconsistency, one that won't end up with the result of not running at all nor with the result of running scheduled marathons.

o

Made a left on Bull Hill Road. I am pretty far from home, up in Western Massachusetts. This road was named after a man named

Bull, not the animal, but it nevertheless serves as a reminder: roads were once for animals at least as much as for people. Animals swerve, whereas humans are expected to angle, though bipedal bodies are no more suited to turning on an angle than four-footed ones are. But angled roads aren't about physiology anyway; they're about property. Establishing a ninety-degree turn to the left by the placement of a road promises a more equal apportioning of land than a slowly curving one, which favors the area of the landholder on the right. I should never forget that my running ways are determined by property. Town planners and lawyers make the path. But runners can create new life on a plane of old macadam.

That's a bit transubstantiation-like, a bit religious. I have just finished reading Jon Fosse's *Septology*, a seven-part novel cycle set in and around Bergen, Norway, narrated by a present-day oil painter who's losing his mind, recounting all that he thinks and does (or doesn't do), amplifying his own narrative with the narrative of another old oil painter with the same name, Asle, who looks like him, lives near him, but instinctively turned right in life where the narrator turned left: the narrator stopped drinking and the namesake did not. You may be reading a delusion, a fantasy, or a metaphor—the narrator is also a convert to Catholicism, and everything's a parable to him. He rescues the namesake from his sad, drunken collapse in the snow one night, brings him to safety and a hospital, takes care of the poor man's dog, all while his neighbor, who is bumptious and poor at reading social cues (the narrator, by contrast, is just monosyllabic, nearly mute), clucks and hems and haws and makes unhelpful comments. That and some inevitable deaths are about the sum of the book's narrative. The rest is a weird brew of memory and moralizing and Catholic liturgy. A wise reader in our family, having already read the book, has been waiting for my report. I told her I liked it a lot but may be forever over my curiosity about Catholic ritual.

Yet now that I am a few weeks and, oh, I don't know, fifty miles past finishing the book, I wonder whether the liturgical recitations that close each part of the novel and the long detours into religious instruction aren't inseparable from the rest of the book. That is to say, if the book's any good, the Catholic teachings need to be there. They seem a mildewy bore to me, as if the reader has to actually lie within the swampy brain of the guy. Precisely, they cross the line from idea into practice—from the great-height vantage of "what this novel is trying to do" to the private, local, locked-in, short-range vision of what a sad man does all day.

I say "short range," but he's touching his rosary beads and thinking about the Catholic god, which is by many definitions the opposite of short-range thinking. Is the joke on him, then?

Perhaps the joke's on me. Fosse himself is a recovering alcoholic and a Catholic; he became those things not too long before I started running. Perhaps what we are getting from him isn't just his disposition; it might also be his zeal. There might not be a difference between the intent and the effect of *Septology*—whose seven hundred pages revolve around the same ten or so characters and the same five or so places, with *much* ritualized repetition—and John Coltrane's last recordings, ten years after he quit heroin and had his own religious awakening. Late Coltrane can sound like one long song, or make you wonder whether you're hearing a song at all, rather than a sustained quality of motion.

A song often has a narrative. Where there is no narrative, there may be, perhaps, no body, no outline, no form, nothing to admire for its shapeliness and symmetry. Yet I seem to be drawn to the promise of a no-song or long-song model for running—the music of both Coltranes, Theo Parrish's long DJ sets, the Fred Astaire–Oscar Peterson trunk sale considered as one unbroken project, and, more recently, pre-baroque music.

I couldn't really (yet) explain to anyone the qualitative difference between the music of Josquin des Prez and Johannes Okeghem, Claudio Monteverdi and Carlo Gesualdo. Sacred works and chansons: maybe I can tell the difference between them— the sacred ones are in Latin and the chansons do moodier things harmonically—but I haven't yet appreciated the ingredients that make each composer distinct. I can barely tell one song from another; I can't tell their landmarks or the aural equivalent of the word "landmark" (which doesn't exist). But it's all a matter of adjusting my hearing.

This is a good place to be in, this place of not quite knowing but wanting to know more.

I have been trying another Renaissance composer, Gilles Binchois, fifteenth-century French Flemish: his work takes up the B-side of a record I bought downtown last week. It turns out that a Belgian vocal group I once saw performing Gesualdo in a twelfth-century church in the Netherlands—the group sang barefoot and you could buy beer in the aisles—made a record of Binchois songs. The group is called Graindelavoix, one word, after Roland Barthes's idea that the "grain" of a singer's voice is the imperfect, bumpy, physical essence of sung communication, the level of singing that can really be heard only as the voice moves, and for which there is little critical vocabulary, because the grain keeps changing. As Nuar Alsadir suggests in her book *Animal Joy*, the grain of a voice does not obey the definition of a single adjective. Is the grain of a voice boring? You could say that—or overgrown, constricting, scratchy, smelly: "blood, saliva, and mucus," she writes, are its causes and analogs. In any case: the grain represents the part of a voice usually deemed less presentable, or less worth bothering with, because it is by definition interior, extraneous, and subject to change according to heat or cold or mood or the temperament of the hour and the place.

Binchois songs, by the Barthes-inspired medievalist singers, are not faceless. They feature distinct voices and grains. Silvie Moors, singing the lead line in "Je ne pouroye estre joyeux," a secular song, uses a disposition that would have been described as folk in the '70s and as pop in the '80s: her wordless vowels tremble in tight coils. Behind her, men harmonize through a collage of throat-grain, some voices nasal and flattened, some round. I am restricted or protected from knowing what the songs are about, as I don't understand Flemish. They are not, in fact, one long song. They're perfectly well differentiated. They don't use the same modes or keys. Yet I hear them as a block. Deaf to their narrative, I tune in to their essence at intervals.

While running, there is no way to remain in any of these songs all the way through, I've decided. This isn't a failure of concentration; it's simply the terms of the contract I've negotiated. If I'm going to hear music while running, I'm going to be in tune with its motion more than its outward shape. I'm going to plunge a sensor inside it, gain some access to the core of it. It's a different kind of "reading" (or the listening equivalent—there is no such word, because "listening" is often understood as passively letting something come to you) from an analysis of choral relationships and lyric scansion. I'm on the run: I'm not looking at sheet music!

In the case of Binchois, there is sheet music, after the fact, though Graindelavoix might like you to pay attention to the parts of the performance that can't be transcribed: the grainy parts. As I listen to them, running on a dirt road through conservation land, I am looking down a wet slope toward the half-thawed Housatonic River and noticing the in-betweenness of everything: weather that isn't quite cold, trees that aren't quite dead, trails that aren't quite clear, woods that aren't quite dense, water that isn't quite frozen. None of it displays a clear narrative. I like music for which there can't really be notation, yet there is at least a recording, despite the encoding, the reduction, and the narrative that a recording produces.

When I listen to music made by a person, as opposed to by nature or artificial intelligence, I like to feel that I am near a person's essence, and I like feeling that I myself, for reasons I have not controlled and did not expect, have been in that person's dragnet. I don't need to be "understood" by the person; I don't need to be loved by the person; I don't need to be known by the person. But I like the feeling that this person might have sensed they'd reach the listening ear of someone like me. So I am listening to them, and because an utterance anticipates a listening ear, they have also been listening to me.

Barthes wrote with his usual capricious performance of mock precision that there were three types of listening: listening for alarms; listening for codes or symbols; and listening that might "develop in an inter-subjective space where 'I am listening' also means 'listen to me.'" Later in that same weird and suggestive essay ("Listening"), Barthes writes:

> To listen is to adopt an attitude of decoding what is obscure, blurred, or mute, in order to make available to consciousness the "underside" of meaning (what is experienced, postulated, internationalized, or hidden). The communication implied . . . is religious: it *ligatures* the listening subject to the hidden world of the gods, who, as everyone knows, speak a language of which only a few enigmatic fragments reach men, though it is vital—cruelly enough—for them to understand this language.

In other words, perhaps, to listen this way is to listen religiously.

// 31 //

The unit of map-measured space I've lived with the most in my life is the neighborhood, and at this stage I don't feel I know any neighborhood until I trace every street and every block of it with my feet. It takes me so long to know a neighborhood— which is to say, to feel close to it or tender toward it—that I wonder what made me feel that way, and only then do I realize what I've done.

My desire to do something similar with music is a little more proactive. I do want to hear music I have not yet heard—I am often writing something or looking for ideas to write about, and the only way to form the ideas is to hear the music, generally from beginning to end. If I am forming an idea about one person's song, I want to hear the song and others related to it, by that person and others: I would like to trace the song's neighborhood. If I am forming an idea about a musician, I want to hear as much as I can by that musician—never in chronological order, but I do keep a rough timeline in my head, thinking about their growth and disintegration. Some of a musician's greatest work happens while they're disintegrating. If time and resources will not allow, that's all right. I can be aware that I don't really know the neighborhood of that musician yet.

Running has a relationship to tracing: going over a previously made shape or pattern that defines a form. I run nearly every day, within the same ten-mile radius. I love the repetition of positive experiences, but at a certain point the love feels shallow, when I don't know the context of the experience, or the area beyond my tracing. When I come to know one route through a landscape, I turn my vision off the path and outward, in the direction of the horizon and contours of the earth; I begin to form a suspicion about where the roads that are around the one I know may lie, and eventually I find myself running on them, if for no other reason than to confirm my suspicions, or to see how good a land surveyor I am. Then, if I travel one of those outside roads, all others will likely follow; it's almost as if they're in pursuit of me. They would like me to know how they fit together. When my tracing is complete, I know the area.

As a runner, what I know best about a route is its gradation: its mild and extreme inclines and declines, the lumbar regions of roads with their sensuous dips, the parts of roads where running suddenly becomes slightly harder, requiring a change in attitude, a shift of mental gears, as well as a change in stride and speed. There is nothing better than hopping slowly up a hill, and there is nothing worse than blasting up the same hill, tapping out before reaching the top. Best of all is that moment of realization, the break in the trance-state, when the incline speaks to me and I make the rational decision to assess what I've got and keep going. As the ATM prompt used to put it, I agree to the fee and I will continue.

Thinking about music that changes slowly, that can't quite be notated, that accretes more than it proceeds, I thought of Éliane Radigue, who has been making slow-change music for more than fifty years. I am impressed and puzzled by her music, have surely heard less than half of it, and that which I have heard

I likely haven't heard in full. I would declare strong feelings for her music, but limited ones, because I do not know her neighborhood. For example, I have a feeling that this musician refuses to accept the normal artist's narrative of growth and disintegration. I can't say why I have that feeling, but I do. And if that's true about her, that refusal is something I would like to feel tender toward.

On a cold and dark afternoon, still in Massachusetts, I run with her *Jetsun Mila*, a recording that has only recently been offered as one eighty-four-minute continuity: it was once separated into two sections, for the convenience of having the work on a two-CD set. It's a good length for the as-yet-unknown-to-me route I will trace, which includes, excitingly, a long stretch of street called Between the Lakes Road. Because I am staying at a house near the top of a hill, it stands to reason that there will be some inclines between me and the lakes.

It is colder than yesterday, low forties, near the line of discomfort for running without gloves. I have no gloves, and just a bandanna covering my head. The days can be dramatic here in the winter months, just as they can be soft and gentle in the summer. The wet rot of the woods and the mouse-colored sky render the cheer of the big houses by the main roads and the scrappiness of the small houses by the lakes as pitiable in the same way. An intense afternoon, and I'm glad to have chosen Radigue for it, because her music seems to emulate the vastness and unknowability of nature. One might want to listen to it under the best possible conditions—a good sound system in a small room, with speakers positioned such that you can hear the dimensions suggested by the music and the flickers of signal in it, all that. But we don't have those conditions, and it doesn't matter too much.

The journalist Kate Molleson interviewed Radigue recently at Radigue's apartment in Paris, in the fourteenth arrondissement, where she has lived since the early 1970s; she knows her own neighborhood well. Radigue told Molleson that she prides herself on having an excellent sense of direction, such that she can find her way around any city without a map, except Venice. "Venice was the only place where I ever got lost," she said, "and that was an incredible feeling." I thought of John Coltrane, who said something similar about his own playing: "I start from one point and go as far as possible. But, unfortunately, I never lose my way. I say unfortunately, because what would interest me greatly is to discover paths that I'm perhaps not aware of." Radigue's music, essentially, brings the map closer and closer to your face, until your expertise at recognizing landmarks is no longer of use. You have to learn a new navigational facility.

Jetsun Mila represents the life of the eleventh-century Tibetan yogi Milarepa in nine chapters. Each of the nine chapters takes time to establish itself before cross-fading into the next. As far as I know, it was made entirely with her ARP synthesizer—an instrument about the size of an old wooden radio console—and a tape recorder. I am not sure if she used prerecorded sound as well as the drones made by her synthesizer. There's plenty of motion in each of the drones, more motion created by her stacking of them, her cross-fading, and whatever else may be there that I do not recognize.

Right away I notice two things. One is that this slow, elegant music may be dangerous to listen to while running on a road: embedded in the sound are blowings and rustlings and various frequencies that sound like trucks at some distance, or sometimes tractors, cowbells, crickets, and planes, also always at some distance. (In her twenties, she lived not far from the Nice airport—presumably the right distance to hear the inclines and declines of takeoffs and landings as music rather than as a nuisance.) Any number of these buried sounds could trick me into the wrong kind of response to a real-time event. If Radigue gives me the sonic approximation of a car driving away to the right, I won't be aware of a real car approaching me on the right. So I am doing a lot of Barthes's first-position listening: awareness of threat or alarm. That is a ridiculous listening position for music this patient, this nondisruptive, and that seems to be teaching you wisdom, and teaching you to relax into the long view (or the listening-vocabulary equivalent of the phrase "the long view," which does not exist).

The other is the fact that a great amount of *Jetsun Mila* uses at least one continuous frequency, regardless of whatever other gapped or repeated or incidental sounds are going on around it. And the continuous frequency changes slowly: it gives the impression of rising and dipping, even if the changes are in timbre rather than in pitch. So the motion of the music is uncannily like feeling the gradation of the road on foot at six miles per hour.

How does she do it? None of the sounds on this enormous work are explicitly of human origin; you don't hear them and picture the person making them. But they must be. Some long tones, about sixty minutes in, sound like men chanting heterophonically. Ten minutes later, that massed sound, seemingly vocal, has turned into something else—perhaps double-reed instruments and low brass. Yet the sounds aren't human; they can't be. Surely they're the creation of the synthesizers, some timbral combination she stumbled onto. They can't be; they must be. It's all human; none of it is human—this music always proposes something in between, parahuman or ghostly. It doesn't matter, because it can't be known: the music teaches the listener to let go.

The place in between, where the body meets the spirit, remains attractive to a runner. That state can't be accessed in the first steps, the first miles, but it certainly can on a *Jetsun Mila*–length run. As with the Éliane Radigue conundrum, how strange it is that the moment of the body's greatest strength becomes the moment of the body's disappearance. After making my way between the lakes, turning toward home base, I am sweating cold into the bandanna, and I can hear my footfalls; I'm feeling the pleasant state of disorientation and desperation. By another way of thinking, I might consider stopping, but what's the point? I'd like to get home and I'm enjoying falling apart.

I am, meanwhile, tracing at least this much of Éliane Radigue's music, which feels good—that's what it's there for, to be used in real time as an agent of disorientation—I am expanding or accreting along with it—I am further tracing the area—I know considerably more about it than I did three days ago.

There must be a better word than "trace." I have only two analogous images in mind for what I'm doing. One is ground-level Google Earth cameras taking their photographs on every street possible for global positioning—an image I don't like much, an activity with built-in complications that are not my own. The other is *Pac-Man*, in which the only goal of the player is to travel all the untraveled pathways on the screen and eat the pellets in its way (while avoiding predators), thereby gaining points and power. But that image doesn't take into account the disappearance or semisacred physical lessening that happens during the process of running. The fact is that, as I go, I am eating up the pellets of the routes unknown to me—yes, I am—and gaining a sort of spatial understanding: the routes become part of my insides. But I am also leaving bits of myself along the road.

The annihilation of the physical and the accretion of the spiritual is what I am looking for—even as I continue to deny the spiritual, even as I doubt it. The edge between resistance and willingness, incredulousness and desire, is where I would like to be. Likewise, my appreciation of this music by Éliane Radigue—I would urge it on people, I would prescribe it—lives in the region of "No! Really? No! Really?"

// **32** //

Issues of proximity are a major theme in city living—they regulate your daily rounds, your share of light and air, your social life, your net worth, your ability to concentrate. (At this moment I am hearing someone nail something into the wall on my left, possibly one flight up but I can't be sure; they swing the hammer in patterns of fours or fives, never threes or sixes.) Sometimes a closeness doesn't register at all, which is its own kind of proximity issue: one often cannot detect what is right beside them. For example, Miles Davis's grave site seemed psychically very distant from me until I realized I could run to it in forty minutes—at least to the perimeter of the cemetery, then walk the rest of the way, because one oughtn't run in a cemetery.

For another example: My father, in the late 1950s, worked in his art school's studio space in Manhattan's East Village, nearly across the street from the Five Spot Café, where for six months in 1957 Thelonious Monk and John Coltrane played six nights a week, four sets a night, subtly reshaping downtown cultural life and, to some extent, their own musical tradition. If my father had thrown a football from the roof of that building—he could throw a football pretty well—it might have landed more than halfway to the Five Spot. But he never knew what was going on inside the Five Spot, because he never converged with it; he never went in there. It's difficult but not impossible to understand: in the narrowest conception of his neighborhood—bounded, let's say, by St. Marks Place to the north, Third Avenue to the east, Houston Street to the south, and Broadway to the west—there might be three thousand doorways. To a newcomer, a doorway is a doorway. None of them in and of themselves will help you realize where you are or who you are. If they're all relative, or if you don't care which one calls to you most, the world decides for you—you experience the world as a drifter. In a place like the East Village in the late 1950s, drifting could be dangerous. You needed to know where you were going. He might have had four or five places to go—who knows, but a limited number. He wasn't going to drop in anywhere by chance, and he might never have grasped the importance of the Five Spot simply by walking past it, as he surely did most days. One creates intention, value, meaning only by moving toward a place; moving past it isn't enough.

o

I'll move slowly here. Two of my favorite musicians lived near each other in the southwest Bronx from the late 1940s to the early 1960s. Or really three: the tres player Arsenio Rodríguez, born in Matanzas, Cuba, in 1911; the pianist Elmo Hope, born in New York City in 1923; and the pianist Thelonious Monk, born in Rocky Mount, North Carolina, in 1917. Rodríguez's primary residence for much of the time he lived in New York was in East Harlem. But he often stayed with his brother Kiki in the Morrisania neighborhood of the Bronx. Morrisania, an area of striving Caribbean and Puerto Rican and Cuban postwar immigrants, and the adjacent neighborhood of Longwood, produced an almost unreasonable amount of bedrock American music in the middle of the century—Afro-Latin, jazz, doo-wop, hip-hop—before the quick and devastating destruction of its population through arson and neglect in the 1980s. Among the great capitals of twentieth-century American music, there are New Orleans and Detroit and Harlem and Chicago and Los Angeles and Kansas City and Memphis and also, though a chamber of commerce has never really claimed it, Morrisania. It is a shadow capital.

After 1948, Arsenio Rodríguez often lived with Kiki on Tinton Avenue near 160th Street. He is known also to have lived on Kelly Street, a ten-minute zigzag from Tinton, and his brother Raúl owned a restaurant between the two locations.

The non-converging proximity of Monk and Rodríguez concerns me most, but Elmo Hope is part of the diagram.

Hope, from the late 1940s through the 1960s, lived on Lyman Place near 169th Street in Morrisania, with his Antiguan mother and (starting in 1961) his wife, Bertha, and new daughter, Monica. This same short block had been familiar to Thelonious Monk since 1942, when his oldest friend from childhood, James "Sonny" Smith, moved there; Sonny's sister was Nellie Smith, who eventually became Monk's wife. So Monk's oldest friend became his brother-in-law, and from the early 1940s onward, Lyman Place in the Bronx became an extension of the Monks' primary neighborhood in Manhattan (West Sixty-Third Street, the Phipps Houses, where Monk's mother lived).

Elmo Hope and his family became part of the Monks' family picture as well, if not part of the family per se. There is the official record of fact—the static certainty of who belongs where and to whom, who has deeds and titles to a certain place and a certain person at a certain time—and there is the version of life brought about by movement and action. This second version is what interests me here.

Monk and Hope had known each other since the early 1940s through New York's jazz orbits. They were parallel originals, co-conspirators, no threat to each other. In 1961, when Monk and Nellie's apartment on Sixty-Third Street was destroyed by fire, Monk and his family took shelter with Nellie's sister Skippy on Bristow Street in Morrisania, a few blocks from Lyman, for the better part of a year, and Monk was known to spend a lot of time with Hope on their stoop; he was in effect living in the neighborhood. In short, Monk's primary residence was on West Sixty-Third Street in Manhattan, but he also lived on Lyman Place in the Bronx.

A memoir published in 2020 by the writer jennifer jazz, who grew up just west of Lyman Place, closer to Yankee Stadium, casually mentions that Monk lived on Lyman Place. How did she know? Her father was a jazz drummer. A guild circulates news of its members. According to Robin D. G. Kelley's biography, Monk and Nellie divided Thanksgiving and Christmas between West Sixty-Third Street and Lyman Place. In some cases, the question of where someone lives becomes academic.

Thelonious Monk and Arsenio Rodríguez did not come from the same musical tradition, but they have some biographical correspondence, and their music appeals to the body in similar ways. Their surviving recordings start at around the same time: 1940 for Rodríguez and 1941 for Monk. The year 1947 was crucial for both: it was the year of Monk's first record under his own name, and his first appearance at the Village Vanguard; it was also the year of Rodríguez's first trip to New York, to meet an eye doctor in the hope that his blindness could be cured—a vain hope, as it turned out. During that visit, he stayed in Morrisania and was feted repeatedly by Cuban musicians, who likely needed him as their mentor and conscience so Afro-Latin music could have a fighting chance: something was just about to happen with the mambo. Within the next few years, before Rodríguez returned to New York in 1950, mambo developed into a culture, and then became an international success that was both authentic and glib, a kind of meme.

Rodríguez and Monk were big men with dark glasses who came down heavily on their instruments, and made flexible, surprising music, full of stylish imprecision. They bore into repetition on small phrases, long trains of notes moving upward or downward, and the crunch and smudge of chords containing slight dissonance. They were indwellers. They could imply a frenetic feeling, but weren't especially fast players; their music so evidently came from their interiors, not their fingertips. ("Evident" and "evidence" come from the Latin *videre*, "to see," and have no equivalents in the language of listening.)

Monk was famous for leaving his piano stool and dancing. If you have seen a big person dance gracefully and with decisive style, you might recognize the sensation when hearing Rodríguez play the tres. Elmo Hope was small and slight by comparison. But he, too, in his playing, made you aware of interiors. Hope's style often forgoes the obvious. He makes abrupt shifts in harmony and rhythm, lets a figure hang unresolved, gets ahead of himself, or fills in a space with a jolt and a bump rather than a nicely rounded phrase.

I have been running through Morrisania and Longwood with about twenty minutes of Hope's music, twenty minutes of Monk's, twenty minutes of Rodríguez's. I'm listening to Elmo Hope's "B's

A-Plenty," from a 1959 trio record, medium up-tempo, with the bassist Jimmy Bond and drummer Frank Butler. Its theme begins before the "one," as if he's breaking early out of the starting block, and continues with a string of feints and trickling misdirections before the sly, complicated line starts again. When he gets to the solo—the rest of the tune is almost entirely his solo—he spends a strangely long time up at the ceiling of the piano's range, the upper third of the keyboard, not particularly thinking about balance or a narrative arc. He begins to play very lightly, as if he'd forgotten the occasion—a recording session, a chance to create something permanent. You sense he couldn't be happier. He's engrossed. Phrases end by flying away into a smudge, or find steadiness in a long tremolo. He has the uncanny alertness of Cecil Taylor, another great maker of running music—with both of them, you feel the force of a note's gesture before the note.

Monk makes even more distinctive asymmetries than Hope, and he is also a subtracter: many of his songs, and certainly his solos, reduce to a basic unit of functionality, like a three-legged stool, but painted in colors that shout across the room. I'm listening to Monk's "Criss-Cross," from 1962. His accompanying chords to Charlie Rouse's saxophone solo are as declarative as any solo can be; when he arrives at his solo, he, like Hope, gives off the feeling of a musician who doesn't need to make anything definitive or "unique" or shaped into a story: he stops, considers, removes himself for a few seconds, and keeps sketching, with a heavier hand than Hope's.

Rodríguez's instrument, the guitar-like tres, is tuned in three sets or "courses" of two strings, each pair tuned either in unisons or octaves, such that any individual double-stringed note produces a piercing sound. His innovation was to create a newly danceable version of the son, the African-influenced style that originated in eastern Cuba, with a small-group instrumentation including two trumpets and a piano. His forceful tres playing functioned like rhythmic and melodic scaffolding for the group; his tres patterns, electrified through a cranked amplifier, commanded you clearly and slowly to move in precise ways, but not necessarily the ways prescribed for mambo dancers in New York in the late '40s. I'm listening to "La Gente del Bronx," Rodríguez's song about his adoptive neighborhood, celebrating the Bronxite willingness to dance. He recorded it twice, in 1953 and 1966. His tres assumes a secondary role in the earlier one—he doesn't take a proper solo—but every time the voices and trumpets clear away, you hear his fingers on the strings, forcefully pushing the vamp forward. The later one is slower and louder, without horns, just Rodríguez's blaring, electrified tres. The motion in Rodríguez's music is pre-mambo, hard to articulate through instruction, hard to commodify, hard to sell. "With Arsenio you had to dance by *feeling* his music," the mambo dancer Horacio Riambau told the scholar David García. "If the dancers didn't *feel* his music . . . they looked like they were foreign because they didn't interpret the rhythm that they played, they didn't carry it inside them."

All of them—Monk, Rodríguez, Hope—carry Caribbean motion in their playing. None of them let their genre or style of music make the decisions for them. They track through it with decision. They don't hide in their music, and you can't miss them.

Hope and Monk, in the 1940s, often played at Club 845 on Prospect Avenue in Morrisania, the best jazz club in the Bronx, and were known to return there during Monk's extended Bronx period in 1961 to hang out, if not perform. Arsenio Rodríguez, in his later and most mystical New York phase, during the 1960s, to the extent that he was known at all was known as an under-appreciated pioneer and prophet, a stout, blind Cuban Jehovah's Witness who identified as African. If, during that period, he had left Kiki's house on Tinton to work at the Club Cubano Inter-Americano on Prospect Avenue—the social club he belonged to, where dark-skinned old-timers like him felt welcome, where he often performed—he would almost certainly have walked two blocks west, crossing Union Avenue to get to Prospect. He would either have passed directly by or been within earshot of Club 845.

Afro-American jazz and Afro-Latin music were intermixed from the start, and remixed at points by specific people in specific places for specific ends; this has created a musical synthesis for which there was no equal in the twentieth century. But not everyone could do this mixing programmatically, or had the means to, or wanted to. Working musicians in popular culture please their audiences; they're not academic about it. Dizzy Gillespie became fascinated with Cuban rhythm because he had Cuban friends in New York who showed him how it was done. He might have had the sort of genius that led him to massage Cuban elements into a North American art form, but it really happened only because in 1941 he moved toward a specific place, the Park Plaza, at 110th Street and Fifth Avenue in Harlem, and sat in with a specific band, Machito and his Afro-Cuban Orchestra, at the invitation of a specific person, the trumpeter Mario Bauzá. He interpreted the music with his own body. And many such visitations from one style to the other happened more frequently later on, based on the knowledge that Gillespie had already done it.

Especially in a place like Morrisania, where live music was for local residents more than for visitors and tourists, Black American music and Puerto Rican music and Cuban music mixed profoundly with one another; leaders of these styles appeared at the same clubs and sometimes on the same concert bills. Plenty of Monk's tunes translate easily to the Afro-Cuban clave rhythm. One of them, recorded for Prestige in 1952, has a particularly distinct clave. Its name was suggested by a Spanish-speaking employee of Prestige: he thought it should be called "Vaya" ("Go"). It became "Bye-Ya."

There are other ways that Monk and Rodríguez can be brought together after the fact. Much as Monk stood apart from bebop— the eventual overtly commercialized version of the musical concept he came from—so did Rodríguez stand apart from mambo, the hip and glamorous version of mid-twentieth-century Afro-Latin dance music. He felt it beneath him. "We are possessed by mambo mania," he complained to an interviewer in 1952. "I was the Dr. Frankenstein who created the monster, and now that same monster wants to kill me." In the early 1960s, by the Cuban standards of the time, Rodríguez played old-man's music: a religious, working-class, dark-skinned old man's music. It was strong and graceful and dancerly and also, toward the end, torrid and noisy. During the '50s, the peak years of mambo, he was not hired in Midtown Manhattan clubs, presumably because he didn't look or sound chic. To see his name in an old New York newspaper dance-palace advertisement, billed under a popular mambo bandleader like Tito Rodríguez, produces a version of the historical dissonance one might feel seeing Buddy Guy open for the Rolling Stones.

So he played where Cubans and dark-skinned people went: the same Park Plaza in East Harlem; Gem's Paradise in Crown

Heights, Brooklyn; the Tropicana in Morrisania. Likewise, well into the 1950s Monk's music was often understood outside of musician circles as eccentric clumsiness. Monk didn't publicly complain much, but he was a Dr. Frankenstein, too, and his friends sensed he was hurt by seeing others becoming synonymous with the musical argot that he'd done as much as anyone to create.

Regarding Rodríguez and Monk, a listener, or a musician, or a dancer, or a runner, might guess that they came from the same tree simply because that tree was stuck so deeply into the center of Black music. Here, a strange coincidence: a passage I read in this morning's *New York Times*, where the writer Ed Morales quotes the Cuban percussionist Pedro Martinez.

"I've seen a lot of Thelonious Monk videos, and he looked a lot like a rumbero," Martinez said, referring to the way Monk would sometimes perform a spinning dance that suggested Yoruban dance and spirit possession. "He stood up to dance and played the piano with one hand and then the other. Jazz has a very spiritual connection to Afro-Cuban music, because it's a way of feeling, of giving reverence to the ancestors."

Their proximity to Prospect Avenue, in the nocturnal watches between Club 845 and the Club Cubano Inter-Americano from the late 1940s to the early 1960s, is enough reason to suggest that Rodríguez and Monk breathed the same air, walked in the same tracks. Surely they would have seen each other. Who, seeing either Rodríguez or Monk approach on the street—or perhaps even *hearing* them approach—wouldn't notice them? But it is not known whether Thelonious Monk and Arsenio Rodríguez ever visited each other in their houses; nor is it known whether they heard each other play; nor has it ever even been proved that they knew about each other.

o

One can't construct a relationship among them based on facts. But one can propose the impossible dialogue—remembering Víkingur Ólafsson's phrase about Debussy and Rameau—through motion, which might be the basis of their connection, anyway.

I have been running through Morrisania with about half an hour of Rodríguez's music and half an hour of Monk's, starting in Crotona Park. *Vaya.* The motion generated by Rodríguez's and Monk's rhythms and tonal resolutions is clear and does not require an explanation; and it is also strange, non-negotiating, big, and full of nonstop presence. The songs and the intentions are sturdy and true, but the notes inside them are all a little crooked, so imperfect that the music will accept you, whoever you are. Perhaps it is dance music for nondancers. Both of them, through their music, encapsulate in a similar way a paradox that may occur to a runner. One runs to simplify, to create clarity, to shed or to become transparent, to disintegrate, to become a stock form of human life. At the same time, when one runs, one picks up more and more perceptions along the way, the senses are flooded, the keen experience of running through a particular place and at a particular hour, and of having particular thoughts on a particular thesis, can make one feel extremely complex, full of peculiarities, possibly unlike any other.

I move southwest along Boston Road, east on 169th, and south again on Tinton to Kiki's address. Switching over to Prospect, I run past the sites of Club 845 and the Club Cubano Inter-Americano and up toward the Hopes' old block. Then back into the middle of Crotona Park via Skippy's block on Bristow and the urban ranch houses of Charlotte Gardens. (Measured another way, the path from Rodríguez to Monk and Hope is also the path between the two major subway stations in the area—the Prospect Avenue station and the Freeman Street station.)

All this area lies within old Morrisania, a two-thousand-acre estate owned in the 1700s by the aristocratic Morris family—from Wales, originally, though they gave up an estate in Barbados for the Bronx—who let dairy farmers lease parts of their land. Lewis Morris, lord of the manor, one of the signers of the Declaration of Independence, argued in Congress in 1790 that Morrisania should be the site of the nation's capital. Not only, he reasoned, was it convenient to ships from the eastern and southern states, its entries by water unimpeded by ice; not only was it surrounded by New Englanders to the north and New Yorkers to the south-west, who were all ready to fight, as opposed to sections of the country with nonfighting Quakers and "negro inhabitants who not only do not fight themselves, but by keeping their masters at home, prevent them from fighting also." But in Morrisania, he proclaimed, "the fever and ague is unknown," and "persons from other places, emaciated by sickness and disease, there shortly re-cover and are speedily reinforced in health and vigor." It was, as he saw it, a protected place; a place to which the news from far-away places could be quickly brought; a place to heal. To a degree, Rodríguez and Monk saw Morrisania that way too.

Morrisania's original parcel of land extended down to Mott Haven and up to Highbridge; the part of it I run on, the center of the landmass, is flat, with the diagonals of Boston Road and Franklin Avenue passing through the quiet streets, resulting in crosshatches or crisscrosses, anvil-shaped apartment buildings and, here and there, short blocks abutting into a perpendicular. The clubs have left Prospect Avenue, now wide and loud with sounds of cars and the overhead subway. Now one sees churches, bodegas, a nail business here and there, and not much else. This is a struggling neighborhood even by Bronx standards. Thin young men in threes and fours, walking quickly down the side streets. Older men in threes and fours talking outside stores. And people on their own, who don't stand out in any New York way, deep in their own calculations, preoccupied. Nobody else is running here, but I attract little attention. I have the feeling I do not exist.

I notice that both Kiki Rodríguez's block of Tinton and Elmo Hope's block of Lyman are like refuges, quiet places to stop and talk or to be uncommon and interior. I notice that Kelly Street, too, has a similar protected feeling.

Perhaps Monk didn't actively align himself with Afro-Cuban musicians by going to their gigs and sitting in with their bands, as Dizzy Gillespie did. But various Latin and jazz musicians did that work later, particularly by transferring Monk's tunes into clave rhythm. They were arranging their kindred forces into proximity, as many artists do with the forces that are important to them, like assembling an altar. Eddie Palmieri, the Latin-music pianist and bandleader, listened closely to Monk in the late 1950s. He had grown up in the '30s and '40s on Kelly Street; his father ran a candy and ice cream store on Kelly at the corner of Longwood where he worked as a soda jerk while commandeering the jukebox. He might have crossed paths with Monk, too, without knowing it. (They properly met only once, in the 1960s.) Through his customers at the store, Palmieri likely understood music as a series of encounters—people and places and records—and when he describes his life, he does so by tagging the people and places and records, laying his magic stones in their proper constellation. I realize I am doing something similar, making these three people the legs of a stool or, even better, arranging them along a route and running among them, trying to make a binding and stable energy arise, tracing the terrain that connects them all.

In another coincidence of proximity, Monk and Rodríguez, who did not know each other in life but to a certain way of thinking should have, are near each other in death. Both are buried at Ferncliff Cemetery, in Hartsdale, New York, in southern Westchester. Their remains are positioned about the same distance from each other within the cemetery, proportionally, as they lived from each other in the Bronx. One would not run between them, because one ought not run in a cemetery, but one can secure the connection by walking.

// **33** //

The narrator of Ice Spice's song "Munch (Feelin' U)" acts out her restlessness within the two opening lines: the first is a skeptical question directed to her pursuer; the second already puts him down in the third person. The video for the song was shot in St. James Park, in the Fordham area of the Bronx, which, she suggested in a recent interview, should be renamed Munch Park. I like to run through Munch Park in the morning, passing the Jerome Park Reservoir on the way, and think about her cool, cosmopolitan equanimity.

Ice Spice's voice—the lightness and control of her tone and timbre and delivery, the half-interested glide in her mode of address—contains persistence reduced to its hardened form (persistence so hard it barely seems like persistence; form so hard it barely seems like form). She doesn't need to blow smoke. When she says "damn" as an interjection, she doesn't even emphasize the word.

The value of her voice lies in hearing it go, not so much in any settled quality. Descriptors fail it. Is it subtle? As one of my students pointed out after class the other day, no, that's not quite it. Affectless? No. Confidential? Intimate? No. Writing can't do much to convey it. If one doesn't hear the voice while it is in motion, it may as well not exist. It may help to be in motion oneself as well.

The nineteenth-century American phrase "admit of" is rarely

used anymore. But even twenty years ago you used to come across it. "Admit of" implied a mixture of airs and nuanced real talk. If you admit an audience to your show, it's business: you're letting them in by means of an exchange—they've given you money, or a promise that they'll behave, or something like that. If you admit a truth, you're simply giving voice to a fact. To admit *of* something is philosophical: you are allowing for the circumstances of its possibility. In the negative, the phrase is always "does not admit of"; to write "didn't admit of" would lessen the majesty of the expression.

In *The Age of Reason*, Thomas Paine wrote that a certain passage from the book of Job "contains two distinct questions that admit of distinct answers." Walt Whitman in a letter to Hugo Fritsch: "The hot weather here does not admit of drinking heavy drinks, & there is no good lager here." Arlene Croce in 1965: "[Fred] Astaire's style, for forty years a major criterion of masculine elegance the world over, does not admit of further definition." Harry Crews, in 1990, on the subject of his love of watching track-and-field athletes, particularly sprinters: "I think all of us are looking for that which does not admit of bullshit."

The entire sounded being of Ice Spice does not admit of bullshit—she doesn't have time, has other things to do, doesn't need to be a virtuoso when simply talking is enough, and I'm sorry, *who are you*? She will be with us for only two minutes. Her songs are so short—like breaths. A person running, similarly, can't and needn't keep stopping to consider the details. The dead-eyed expression sets in, the equanimity and resistance to interruption. To be doing something so extravagant with your body without bothering (or even interesting) anyone, without endangering yourself: Is it not like, say, flying?

Her speed and stamina and reserve might come down to breath control. Like a runner, or like a dancer on the order of Suzanne Farrell, she's not counting her rhythms, not saving up big gulps or exhalations for the allotted spaces. She keeps a reserve of air in her chest and lets only a tiny bit out. One imagines her upright with her shoulders back, holding herself lightly but alertly. Like Astaire as a singer, Ice Spice is not a particularly "good" rapper, but possibly a great one.

As I run, I listen to the songs on her first EP in order and then on repeat. They're over before you know it. She's passing through, even faster than I am. They're perhaps not ideal for long vistas, but they are right for their point of origin. How to explain this feeling of gotta-go? Her home neighborhood, Fordham, is full of that energy: the elevated train on Jerome Avenue cuts through it, the major artery of Kingsbridge Road cuts the other way, and the old aqueduct lies just east of Jerome; old military, civic, and educational institutions dot the area. The place admits of ambition, institutions that get you from one place to the next, but in a larger sense there's not a lot going on. It might be music to propel you forward, to get you out of where you've been.

// 34 //

With earphones, your devices for listening are in fact "in your head," inserted directly into two of your head-holes. But this way of listening also invites you to experience music as a cousin of non-sounding brain activity, like memory or dreaming. Music can get a bit less objectively "real" by listening to it through earphones, and in a pretty attractive way, because you might be filing the heard experience very close to wherever you file dreams and memories, and also because nobody else can confirm what you're listening to and how it may be affecting you.

The students I teach often write about "nostalgia" taking a major part in their acts of listening. The use of this term, I think, has grown steadily in the student vocabulary over the last ten years. They listen specifically *for* the feeling of nostalgia: to certain songs that will reliably produce it, certainly, but even without the benefit of those triggers, they are listening for the feeling of nostalgia in themselves, even if there is no specific referent. After all, any number of stimuli might unlatch you from the responsibilities of the now and make you suddenly feel more sensitized. The question of whether that has to do with memories of yourself at an earlier age, or of the world at an earlier age, might be beside the point. I wonder whether "nostalgia" is simply becoming a shorthand term for a condition of sensitivity: the pure feeling of emotion, without the gainsaying impulse to modify it into what's practical or productive. And so I don't always know exactly what my students mean—nostalgia for what?—but that's another issue. I have a feeling the condition of nostalgia is easier to access via the effect of listening through earphones. It may be like curing one's anxiety by breathing into a paper bag.

An effective sound mix is one in which different elements of sound coexist to form a pleasing unity. Or, to put it another way: an effective sound mix is one in which different elements of sound convey the impression that they have been arranged for the same purpose by a presiding conscience—the drum sounds are *supposed* to live alongside the keyboard sounds, varied though they may be. It doesn't matter whether any or all of those sounds are created in an open acoustic space or through the circuitry of a digital instrument: they cohere, and they suggest a coherent space of music.

I have been paying attention to a band that suggests a completely incoherent aural space: the English band Dry Cleaning. I'll try to explain this as simply as possible. The musicians in the band are making acceptably moody, rugged post-punk using the standard instruments for the job (electric guitar, bass, a drum set), playing through amplifiers in a recording studio; you can imagine them doing this, being together. You don't *have* to know they are all together in the same room, which in fact they are (except for the drummer, Nick Buxton, who plays in a sound booth with a glass door facing the others); simply, together-in-a-room is what almost every record by a band implies. But the band's vocalist, Florence Shaw—in the way she conceives of a vocal performance, and by the logic of the sound mix as one hears it—is not in that room with the band. She may not even be in the same city or country, or week or year, with them. Her relation to the music can seem like the relation of someone reading ad copy to the commercial jingle that underlies it.

The history of talk-singing is often told as a line connecting operatic *Sprechstimme*, the folk-style "talking blues" numbers of the 1950s and 1960s; dub-reggae declaiming by Big Youth and others in Jamaica, and Mark E. Smith's slightly later version of the same with the band the Fall. But there are other precedents too. The way Florence Shaw talk-sings relates to the "recitation" parts of slow country songs from the '50s and '60s, like Kitty Wells's 1953 "I Gave My Wedding Dress Away," when singers step out of the tune and read a kind of tale or homily, for the length of a chorus, while the band plays on. Shaw's practice might also relate to Suzanne Vega's original "voice in your head" sound in songs from the 1980s like "Marlene on the Wall," in which she sings melodies in tune, but quietly, close to the microphone, with no aural smiling.

But Suzanne Vega is absolutely in the song, in the production, and so is Kitty Wells: the tone of their talking agrees with the music underneath it. Shaw is operating more ambivalently. You might expect her to hit similar emotional marks as the guys in her band slugging it out together, but effectively she does not: she talks quietly, collage style, a sharp and funny remark followed by an oblique phrase pointing toward nothing. Some singers learn to be singers by emoting in their bedrooms; she seems like someone who learned by making her internal thoughts external. Funny, not funny: it doesn't matter, as long as it stops time for a moment, disturbs the normal run of things.

From "Driver's Story":

I'm not mad keen on it . . . not a standout for me . . .

From "New Long Leg":

Are you taking a photo, or drinking a bottle of water?
Are there some kind of reverse platform shoes that make you
go into the ground more, make you reach a lower level? Never
mind . . .

I've had trouble listening to Dry Cleaning, perhaps the kind of trouble they want me to have. I find listening to their official recordings nearly impossible: they mix Florence Shaw so high and intimately, in such an inapposite degree to the band, with such a degree of autonomy from it, that I can't quite accept it as integrated with the rest. It sounds like one long ad, or some sort of trick meta-commentary, like a parody voice-over. Sometimes it even sounds like a mistake. But every once in a while Shaw phrases her spoken words in the precise rhythm of the beat, or will sing along to a melodic shape in the song, and this keeps me engaged. I don't know how others hear it, but I think they're doing something counterintuitive and risky.

I have also seen them live, and a different problem arises: Shaw's not miked loud enough, and the problem is that she can't be: because she's speaking quietly, and in a live venue, like the midsize clubs the band plays, it's hard to get the necessary separation from a loud-strumming and-beating band. You've come to the gig for the unlikely turns of her lyrics, and you can't hear them.

I decide Dry Cleaning is in a rare category: an impossible band—a great band, and at the same time a band that cannot be listened to. The band is best in my imagination, as "music in my head," which can always strike the right sound balance—or can strike a balance that need not be defined, because it is not sounded, because it is only in my head. And this makes sense to me because Florence Shaw's voice is—as a persona, a mood, a character type—quite appropriate for the role of the voice in one's head.

As it happens, there is a third possibility for listening to Dry Cleaning. After I'd sorted it as an impossible band, I found that Dry Cleaning recorded a video session at the headquarters of Bandcamp in Oakland. It's about half an hour long, in black and white, a fixed-camera documentation of an in-studio live performance, without distraction: no clapping in-studio audience, no promotional interviews, no host. Between songs, the band members come to a complete stop in their playing and chat a little before continuing. And here in this document Dry Cleaning achieves the sound balance I haven't heard on the records or at concerts. I can hear Shaw clearly most of the time, but not too clearly. I can register how she reproduces the perplexing and familiar cadences both of beneath-notice small talk and the weirdo-subconscious mental notations one might make before or after the small talk.

Her "singing" suggests the realm of what the music and literature scholar Lawrence Kramer calls "the audiable": it is the hearkened but not heard, the expressed but not sounded, the "sound of the wave before it breaks," the "material promise of sound," or the resonance of a finished sound-event below the threshold of audibility that may continue within yourself, or—in some cases—the voice in your head. Florence Shaw makes the audiable audible: that's how she works.

To run with this Dry Cleaning Bandcamp studio session is a rare pleasure, then: it integrates material and commentary, outward rocking and a version of the inward mental chatter I might be carrying on anyway, but this chattering has been made part of the art. It is "emotions" (the austerity and foreboding of the guitar melodies, the fat and determined bass lines) paired with the antimatter of the subconscious. It's so complex, in a way, this full presentation of opposites, that it becomes as complex as the act of running itself: the intensity of the external world and the intensity of the internal world experienced simultaneously, sometimes resulting in moments of crisscross, of one becoming the other, of the two worlds trading places. I'm thinking the trail, I'm running through my mind.

It's a pity Dry Cleaning played for only half an hour at Bandcamp HQ. I could run with that for a few hours, I think. It makes the everyday seem exciting and strange; it sensitizes. It might cause nostalgia. The nonvocal part of it is so workmanlike—so get-the-job-done, these-not-particularly-special-pedals-make-this-guitar-effect-that-you've-probably-heard-before, we'll-be-loading-out-our-own-gear-thanks—that the long backtrail around the local parkland area, where I have run thousands of times, seems honorable.

Because Dry Cleaning forces a listener to come to terms with the space in which music is created, I have to face the fact that I seem to prefer running with music made out loud, acoustically, as it were: not necessarily with nonelectrified or nonelectronic instruments (I don't care; they're all a gift), but by sounding instruments in a real-life sound-space, as opposed to music made with a computer interface. I like thinking about sound in a physical atmosphere, because—just like me, running on a sidewalk or a trail or up a steep hill—it must reckon with circumstances exterior to its making. A *sounded* sound, captured by a microphone, has to confront the realities of the place where the microphone is. (Echoey? Acoustically dead? Picking up tensions between musicians? Too far away from them or too close?) It also has to confront the realities of the microphone: they're all slightly different. Music made directly into software must confront its own issues, but they're essentially issues of coding, not of atmosphere.

Yet I choose to run alone, with earphones stuck in my head-holes, rather than to exercise among others, listening to and interacting with external human factors, in a gym or a pool or a studio. I run alone and in my own world, in the recorded music's dreamlike or memorial or nostalgic time, while listening to those who make music together in a sort of time that can only be now, and now, and now.

// 35 //

A friend of mine, W. A. Mathieu, who goes by Allaudin, has written both the most complex and the most simple books about music and listening that I have ever read or tried to read. He knows a great deal about music—through playing it, listening to it, composing it, building his life around it—and understands it as a force that doesn't exist autonomously but is created inside us. On a video call, I reran my basic idea past him: that music has motion; that motion can suggest an atmosphere. When you yourself are in forward motion through your own atmosphere, you are in a position to understand a certain aspect of what's going on in any kind of music—at least, an aspect stripped of narrative—to such a point that your motion and the music's motion, your atmosphere and the music's atmosphere, can begin to crisscross.

"But when you're sitting perfectly still in a concert hall listening to Beethoven, listening intently, couldn't that also be a kind of motion?" he countered. "Your mind is certainly moving. And you might be better suited to hear all the particulars of what's going on."

Could be. Then—I can't remember what got us to the subject—he started talking about how narrative is everything: everything we do, everything we live. And so there is nothing in music that can't be understood as narrative. Complicate, then resolve: narrative. Home-away-home: narrative. Harmonic relationships, he said, are like breathing: expand, contract.

"So," I asked, "do you mean breathing is narrative?"

"Of course," he said. "As soon as we're born, we're in a narrative. We're trapped in this body and it's going to carry us through the story, however it turns out."

I had a hard time with the part about breathing. Oh, there are all kinds of narratives. But because many of us are predisposed to like and accept narrative, I often worry that some narratives have been made to contain us, to sort us, to move us around more easily, to render us a fact of the past in order to later prove some predetermined point, achieve some end that may be terrible, or against our best interests, because it has little to do with us per se. And the hopeful act of "changing the narrative" might retain some of the characteristics of the useless, older narrative, simply through the insistence that what replaces it should also be a narrative. On the other hand, breathing seems to me about being in the now. A minute or an hour or day of breathing, yes, there could be a narrative imposed there, after the fact. But I'd like to think a single breath doesn't have to *mean* anything; it isn't pointed toward any direction in particular.

Also, as I told my friend, where music is concerned I am usually looking to understand music as it exists with its container off.

"Well, sure," he allowed: "if you step into a jazz club in the middle of a set, there might be a pleasant moment when you haven't yet recognized the tune, or you don't yet know where you are in the song, but pretty quickly you figure it out. Unless it's free jazz, although that can become tiresome pretty quickly."

I had a hard time with this too. He knew whom he was talking to; that's why the conversation turned this way. I like the feeling of not knowing where I am in the song so much that I essentially want to stretch out that feeling in my aural perception, make it last as long as possible, and commit to memory this not-knowing perception of the music as its representative sample.

Then he raised a question that he has raised before with me: Does one become a better writer about music if one knows more about how it works? Is it as simple as that? What's the nature of the relationship there? He knows that my understanding of music has limitations because my playing ability is limited, that there is a kind of practitioner-listening that I can't do.

It's definitely true, Allaudin said, that some very good composers are not at all good writers. But if you won't or can't hear a piece of music, accurately, as a chain of structural relationships—which, inevitably, means *as a narrative*—then are you always falling short of what you could be doing?

The discrete orbital spinning in this conversation reminded me a little bit of Oscar Wilde's dialogic essay "The Critic as Artist." One person, Ernest, praises the value of art and artists, doubts the value of criticism, and defines the nature of the critic as adjunctive. The other person, Gilbert, says a series of things that sound outrageous but usually have some truth to them. He insists that critics can perceive things that artists can't, and even more, that critics categorically advance and broaden art-making by perceiving these things, whereas artists tend to be immersed in their own task, essentially repeating the same thing, only refining it. To some degree they are both right.

My sense, I said, is that the way I want to know any music is from the inside, from a place where I can neither sense nor am particularly concerned with its overall structure; a place where perception of narrative is difficult, either by force of will or not. (I was thinking here about something specific. It's a record made by musicians from the Lobi people in Burkina Faso, made with balafon, shaker, and voice: a lot of routing through a limited set of variations, and a fantastically dense but spacious atmosphere of tone and presence, like a heavy mist. Its liner notes will tell you that the music enables communication with the dead, so a player or a listener can occupy several time-planes at once, and that it typically goes on all day during a funeral process, but you may not need to read that to sense it.) It seems to me that as soon as you're talking about narrative, you're talking about the container, or at least the binding agents that hold the stuff together inside the container, more than about the ingredients.

My discomfort with narrative and "containers" might come from having been trained at a newspaper as an everything-ist, to write about nearly all kinds of music both as sound and as culture, and having no motivation to rank one above another. It might also come from having written more about live performances— where many things are potentially possible and music unfolds in real time—than about recordings, where a great deal of sorting and containing has already been done before the sounds reach your ears. It might also be because I can't follow plot very well, and—I admit—sometimes resent it.

"You can listen to music as if it has no container," Allaudin said. "I did it once," he recalled, "with Beethoven's String Quartet no. 14, when I was on an LSD trip. I got so far inside it that I didn't recognize the sounds as coming from instruments; instead, they were shapes and colors and messages."

"Yeah, but you recognized them as such, didn't you?" I asked. "You, who knew the music well. You brought your own perceptions to that listening experience." He assured me this was not true: there was no "I" listening to the music.

"Understanding a piece of music without containers is an extreme," he cautioned. "Let's say it's on one end of the string. Beethoven's String Quartet no. 14 might be on the other end of the string, because it's so much about narrative. To really know your position, you have to also deal with what's on the other end of the string."

So I am taking Beethoven's String Quartet no. 14 in C-sharp minor, Opus 131 with me on running routes that connect a number of dramatically different kinds of terrain, more than usual, just as the music does. (The work has seven sections, more than any of Beethoven's other string quartets, and he specified that they be performed without pauses.) There are parts of the piece that I become restless with; I experience something like that feeling in various running atmospheres as well, when whatever I'm moving through appears too determined and isn't what I want. There are great differences in tempo and energy and orientation: skipping, gliding, mourning, regimented, free, feeling the body, and feeling the imagination. I'm not particularly bothered by the notion that I'm hearing it through earphones rather than seated in a concert hall and hearing the sounds ring out against the woodwork, because when Beethoven composed it, he had been completely deaf for ten years; this was the sound in his head.

While running to Opus 131, it won't do to let it wash over you. There is a lot here. If it is possible to think about a listening experience as including all the thinking you do about the music *after* you hear it, all the ways you live through it after it enters your body, the experience of listening to Opus 131 is enormously front-loaded. You can do what you want with it in your own processing later on, but in real time it's hard to ignore that the number of composed decisions, on micro and macro levels, represents a whole different order from . . . a lot of other music. It asks and assumes a great amount of you as it moves. Running on new routes can feel arduous; once you run them a sufficient number of times, they're not so arduous. There's nothing to do but to run with Opus 131 repeatedly until it feels familiar, or as close to familiar as it might let me be. Gaining familiarity is a process of memory and pattern recognition, but also, almost inevitably, measurement: the first movement of the piece takes about as long as it takes to run to the right turn where the big fat tree fell over last year. A specific high note becomes associated with a traffic light intersection a mile onward. As I make sense of Opus 131, I am discerning what all its patterns and gestures have to do with one another, and most of the environment I'm running through recedes, except for its landmarks.

From my perspective, Opus 131 is front-loaded within itself too. I am amazed by the first movement, the fugue, so tense and mysterious and ambidirectional, and perhaps full of ideas that are amplified and extended later in the piece (though not explicitly so). The last movement, by contrast, is frenetic, galloping, severe. John Dalley, a violinist in the Guarneri Quartet, described the way it can make a musician feel deranged while playing it: "You want to bark like a dog," he said. Not just from the last movement's specific mood, I imagine, but from the compounded pressure built up through the piece over forty minutes. Its organization as a whole compounds on a high level: I don't really feel decisive turns into new sections. ("Compound" is a word related to financial value; the word may be appropriate for a piece of music that has created a lot of financial value.) No section stands apart; no area says, "Done!" Everything stays; everything gets folded in. Yet over the length of the piece, the quartet moves from the ineffable toward the material. There is a sense, for me, in which the work slowly deflates after the first movement.

It might even begin its deflation in the middle of the first movement. Or sooner. Possibly, the version I have been listening to begins its deflation from the moment when the brain of Frederik Øland, first violinist in the Danish String Quartet, sends a message to his right hand to sound the first note of the first movement. But it's like Alice Coltrane's moments of diving in: if one likes that millisecond when the hand comes down, maybe one can somehow expand the essence of it and live in it. And it's like what a friend once said about Fred Astaire: that in his movies he is greatest when standing still, because at all such moments he may begin to dance.

o

The start of Opus 131's opening adagio, with its solitary violin, full of doubt and hesitation, follows some logical downward stepwise movements: this might be running down the hill toward Broadway and the great Van Cortlandt field, at the beginning of a day when I am not quite confident, and potentially unsettled by anything. The first violin seems to imply distraction, hauntedness, a state of being less than sure of its destination; the other instruments of the quartet join one by one in the beginning in canonlike sympathy but seem similarly to lose their will. How they join and console one another, toward a different sound and a different feeling, in an arrangement of background and foreground, is not a unitary matter. You can't sum up its disposition, because it keeps growing, always in process, like shifts along the color spectrum; there are no stations, per se, only movement. It climbs and surges in pitch and intensity but doesn't gloat; it demonstrates to you how it works downward and then up again in logical harmonic movements, like the terraced routes in these woods, connected in places by cross-paths with railroad-tie steps at their steepest points.

The very odd thing about this opening movement is how its language of rising and falling, and its enfolded surges and dives (highs that carry within them the anticipation of lows, and vice versa), never quite come to a rest. It proceeds elegantly and gravely, and would seem to use a recognizable language of emotion to establish its relationship with the listener. ("Risking bravery with a worried mind" might be the closest I can get to characterizing its emotional world.) But the relationship is unstable. Resolutions are barely given a second to ring out before the forward pull yanks them onward to the next ambiguous sequence. The piece is a bit like a river in darkness, calm with a strong current. Tender and beautiful from a certain angle, terrifying from another.

o

In 2011 the art critic Peter Schjeldahl gave a lecture at the New School about Wilde's "The Critic as Artist," responding to a writer and a piece of writing he loved from a distance of 120 years. The lecture would be published in Schjeldahl's final book, but the talk that day was filmed and continues to live online. (At the beginning, Schjeldahl says he thinks all lectures should last only twenty minutes, and the timer running along the bottom of the screen shows us that it lasts exactly twenty minutes.) A few minutes in, he runs through a section from his text explaining the philosophy of the character Gilbert, who contends that artists themselves are critics. "'[Gilbert] begins by pointing out that artists themselves function critically, in what they choose to do and not do,'" he reads. "'They are critics narrowly but deeply focused on their own work; their decisions become history.'"

Then Schjeldahl lifts his head up from his script and talks to the audience. His eyeglasses frames are spectacularly bent at the left temple: it must be from all that manipulation of distance, moving back and forth between looking at a painting in the long view and close up, all those instances of taking them off and putting them back on. He offers something a little provocative, in the manner of Oscar Wilde.

"See, even bad art becomes the history of bad art," he says, "which is actually, usually, more telling. I mean, bad art tends to have *very* specific period looks and preoccupations. It thinks it's repeating the good artists of the previous generation, but with certain mistakes which are highly characteristic and instructive. Good art just tells you that you're overwhelmed." He looks back down at the text to find his place again. "It's not as informative."

A person like Beethoven, self-critical and paranoid though he was known to be, must have had a sense of himself as equal to or maybe even greater than a revered statesman. Perhaps his circle had only one center. The culture of his music came to him: the developing worlds of concert-hall listening and music publishing built up in the shape of his work and thinking. He must have known that every move or decision he made in his music would be attended to. Perhaps he was as self-conscious a representation of the idea of history as music ever had.

And perhaps that's why running with Opus 131 isn't easy for me, despite the skipping and galloping and racing parts of it. It's good art; it also carries a strong sense of itself as and within history. I may be running in part to become overwhelmed, and therefore to slip out of criticism, and out of history.

// 36 //

Another way to look at the narrative-or-not-narrative question is that both conditions can coexist. For my running I often return to a particular set of recordings when I neither feel intentional design in my life, nor am I determined to go the other way, to willfully step out of history. They're by Sonny Rollins.

In 1959—I know this story and am wary of how easily I can recount it—the saxophonist Sonny Rollins, nearly thirty years old, sought a break from his routine of performance and public visibility. In the preceding years he had been recognized and celebrated in the jazz scene in general as a prizewinner, a poll-topper, a standard-bearer, a next step in aesthetic evolution, the fastest and smartest and most heroic player of an instrument conducive to heroic behavior. He'd also been described, by the critic Gunther Schuller, as a musician with an uncanny ability to construct improvised solos that announce their own form as they unspool. He might have enjoyed the attention, but he was bothered by how much this praise didn't square with his own notion of how much work he had yet to do. (I wonder if he felt he was praised for being a confirmer of values that he secretly didn't hold.) So in the spring of 1960 he canceled his phone service and took daily walks through the Lower East Side to a spot on the walkway of the Manhattan Bridge, where he regularly practiced, through the seasons, for up to sixteen hours a day. This extended break perhaps represented a way of stepping out of history and narrative as it was defined by other people, and perhaps a way of slowing down time for himself.

This story, among others, has made Rollins famous as a champion practicer. But practice takes many forms, as various good friends have reminded me at the right moments. Sometimes it just looks like thinking, and sometimes it looks like wasting time, such as looking something up that you may or may not use. Practice as a writer sometimes takes the form of running. Practice as a runner sometimes takes the form of writing. Practice as a listener sometimes takes the form of running or writing—or reading, because prose rhythm, syntactical arrangements, and punctuation create a sound, and to read is to listen to that sound.

When Rollins returned to the public flow of things a year and a half later, his music had a slightly different relationship to narrative. He made a record in January 1962 called *The Bridge*, and his solos on it had more querying hesitation than before. It cast more doubt about flowing rhythm and resolution. He was likely to make the sounds of discontinuity—sputtering, falling silent—with peculiar intent. He formed a new band, with the trumpeter Don Cherry and the drummer Billy Higgins, both from Ornette Coleman's group, alongside his former bassist Bob Cranshaw—and this band played circle-with-many-centers, expectation-frustrating music for two weeks at the Village Gate, on Bleecker Street in Greenwich Village, New York, in the second half of July 1962.

The last four nights of the run were taped at the club by RCA, in the hope that the live performances would yield a live record, more product to meet a projected demand after his return. And they did: the label deemed an album's worth of performances releasable. *Our Man in Jazz* ran forty-nine minutes, unusually long for an LP at the time. An album breaks down into separate tracks with titles. The Rollins quartet's performances that week went on and on and often could not be titled, because they were not songs, per se. Or perhaps it is more fair to say that the selections chosen by RCA for release on the LP were the ones that were most recognizable as songs. They were portions of longer sets full of music made by people who knew about narrative but wanted to turn it inside out.

Beyond the *Our Man in Jazz* material, there were five and a half more hours of tapes from that week, finally released on a set of CDs fifty-three years later as *Complete Live at the Village Gate 1962*. For running, I like to start in the middle of all this middleness—on disks four and five, say—and choose tracks with titles of no significance to me, such as "Untitled Original A #2," eighteen and a half minutes long, which for obvious reasons did not make it onto *Our Man in Jazz*. What happens? Rollins plays a short figure, Cherry plays a figure, they invent an oblique way to play in tandem, with lots of open space and silence. Their collective relation to a home key remains tenuous. A song, such as it is, might amount to a series of stops and starts. A groove emerges for a while, and you hear the moves of Rollins's quick mind. The groove stops unceremoniously. Rollins plays some blips. (By the evident logic of the music, no other musicians need to accompany him, but the choice seems to be up to them.)

As I have my own reactions to this in real time, I like to imagine the audience's. Were they thinking, "This famous person may not be any good"? Were many people wondering whether they knew anything about anything? How many were imagining that their own experience of wandering through this music resembled Rollins and company's, as players?

By habit and preference, Rollins couldn't stay away from quoting tunes of all kinds—anthems, nursery rhymes, Tin Pan Alley songs, bebop themes, classical-music overtures, whatever. At the more commercially acceptable moments of the Village Gate set, such as on the version of "Oleo" that wound up on *Our Man in Jazz*, he practices this quoting game in his usual way. And when I run to this "Oleo," the pulse carries me along; I feel the excitement of the semi-familiar. But deep in the territory of the untitled tracks, he stays away from predetermined melodies almost entirely. Instead, he plays shapes and gestures. At one point halfway through "Untitled Original B," Rollins plays four bars of a blues line; naturally, you expect him to continue it. He doesn't. Cherry reacts in the neighborhood of that blues and that key, but what you hear almost sounds like postproduction, as if his blues response had had gaps inserted into it after the fact by a creative tape-editor. Rollins plays the first three notes of "Taps" and you assume you'll hear the next three, but you don't. He plays the first five of "The Streets of Cairo" and moves on.

This isn't the old Rollins in full; it's a partial glimpse of him, as if he were mostly hidden behind a wall. He achieves autonomy from the band, from the occasion, from the moving sidewalk of the song. He is still practicing on the bridge, as it were, but now in a club. He has consented to play for people. It occurs to me that if you spend a year and half doing something as hostile toward outgoing, transactional, organized show business as cutting off your phone service and playing into wind and traffic noises, you must have a period during that time of honestly wondering whether you want to go back. You must develop a different set of standards about what you're doing and why. I imagine the audience for a Sonny Rollins set in the summer of 1962, faced with this ambivalent music, might think, "Do we still want him?" And I imagine Rollins onstage, thinking with equal force, "Do I still want you?"

I run around my immediate neighborhood with these performances in unbroken amazement. There's no script they're following (other than their conceptual "rules," which I confess I can't recognize in the results), so the music has no inevitably-pulled-forward feeling. It could all fall apart at any second, as they say, but of course it won't, because these people are performers and know about momentum. Regularly, I imagine turning their movements back on myself, or running their song. This recording is not a narrative; it's not a recitation, an account, a version. It's not particularly a protest or a refusal, either. It's much more a question without an agenda, and the question as I translate it might be: Why am I running? Do I want to run? Where am I going? And now? And now? The questions don't defeat me; they feel legitimate and honest. I run every day, and I don't think I would feel any urgency about my practice if I didn't occasionally wonder why I do. Because the music sounds so much like practice, it naturally reminds me of running as practice—not an accomplishment but part of a life's work.

// 37 //

A path invites. As you move toward it, it becomes a suggestion and a direction for further movement. If a runner can expand the idea of the path to the curves of the world seen aerially on a map or sensed by the eye and the foot, then there really is no limit to the invitation.

A running way—let's call it that—accepts you as you are on that day at that hour. The question of "how you are" presumes a range. Even if you eat the same meals every day, even if you go to sleep at the same time, even if your daily rounds seldom change, there are still the seasons, there is still the moon, there is still weather and aging and love and parents and the limits of one's body. And then there are the other variables: not just what you drank last night but what your girlfriend said to you thirty years ago, waves of haplessness or artificial gusto, rare and happy feelings of being returned to yourself, and the rest. To fall asleep is to be unaware of who you might be when you wake up.

At the end of a semester of teaching, colleagues stop in the hallway amid their hustle to talk about how they are fried, ready to stop, can't take anymore, on autopilot, dazed. In May especially: the temperature relaxes their shoulders, makes them breathe more slowly, and they think, "Maybe it's already over? Did I miss the last class? What am I doing at the copying machine? Why am I rushing?" A bit of forgivingness replaces the cold-weather discipline, and we want our students to make it through: Come on now, you've come this far, you can do it, you've done it before—it's already done, as the gospel singers say—just show up and follow through and make your elegant exit.

That's "how I am" on a morning, out on the path or on the way, accepting a purely modular sense of time—let yesterday be yesterday and tomorrow be tomorrow—out in the bright, pale-green, cold, mid-spring atmosphere, a bit aware of how much I have to do, unsure of the precise timing for getting it all done, but then what is "all"? I have no desire or ambition, per se—I'm not going anywhere new today and feel no needs for myself—but I have presence. All right, I'm here. The state I'm describing is a bit rubbed-smooth, non-dynamic, not very exciting, wouldn't you agree? It doesn't really have a name. The path accepts me anyway. In fact, the path is able to remind me I exist, tell me who I am and what I'm feeling, and give it some kind of name. I run as slowly as I want to today, then I come to and realize I'm running fast up a steep hill; I'm barely paying attention, I'm just going on and on as if there were no alternative and thus no possibility of regret. I'm a bit tired and my mind is nowhere and everywhere. It's a good feeling.

O

The musician Keiji Haino spoke to the journalist Alan Cummings sometime in the mid-1990s about the breath-event with which he prepares for a performance:

> Before I make any sounds, first of all I breathe in all the
> air in the performing space. Most performers feed off the

audience, but I'm conscious of entering into a relationship with the actual air in the place, even before the audience has arrived. After breathing in all the air, when I breathe out again I want to engulf the audience in that air. And then on top of that, I want to return the air to its original state again. When I breathe in all that air and engulf the audience in it, it feels like I have become god. That in itself would be blasphemy, which is why I then return the air to its original state. That's the process that I'm always aware of. This might sound like a joke, but it's not—it's easy to become god, but difficult to keep that power. People often say that my sounds are loud, and that can be a negative thing. It's not the sounds that are loud, it's me. I actually become the sounds. People often say how opera singers should sing not from the throat but from the diaphragm, or with their whole bodies. But that just limits the sound to yourself— what I want to do is make the air *itself* vibrate. And that's why it's loud. I give my body to the air.

As a kid I bought a ragged LP of Otis Redding's *In Person at the Whisky a Go Go* at a library sale. The record itself was about my age—maybe thirteen. I had never heard the music before, and it seemed to me, ahistorically, to come from a similar neural frequency and lung capacity as the punk bands I was listening to— it found a level of intensity beyond what one could reach with effort; it required an unreasonable effort, the special reserve of unnameable ability one keeps hidden away within, the siege mentality. But Otis Redding's music seems to be driven by love and yearning instead of anger. I listened to the record so often, not having much of a vocabulary for it, that its details entered my body permanently, as music often does. Certainly Redding's singing did, the way he restlessly patrols a song with his battery of phrases—"hah," "ah nah-nah," "got-ta," "earler in the morning" (always "earler"), "late in the evening," "in the midnight hour," "everybody wants it," "baby, we got it," "I need it"— and also the guitarist, a minimalist ideal, playing just the ropy counter-lines to Redding's vocal melody, mostly on the lower three strings, or often just a slow arpeggio, up and down, up and down, then shoving a stylish triplet phrase into the repetitions, sharp and lean, with trancelike concentration on a task. I picture his legs together, and on the triplets he folds at the knees like an Anglepoise lamp: I don't know the man's name, but I can picture the tailoring of his pants. And the drummer, who has such a job to do, so many parts where every beat of one-two-three-four is splashed, slammed, and emphasized, it's go-go-go, the snare hits go *thwack!* and the kick drum pushes you backward, it's funk drumming but not as tapered as it would be in James Brown's band; it's looser but it doesn't lose its place; it's also *harder* and broader and ruder than James Brown's drumming, yet with details in place for each song, arranged logically and consistently, like a language, a system, the way great musicians do it, and now forty years later I often find myself reproducing the drum parts with my hands or feet or by chattering my teeth: I can play it all and spool out more, new songs with the same style, like an AI program.

The hundredth or thousandth article I read about AI this year made me remember the drumming on the Otis Redding record, so I looked it up: I care about names and dates, but I realized I never knew the guitarist's name (James Young) or the drummer's name (Elbert Woodson), and I never knew exactly when this live album was recorded, at the Hollywood club of the album's name in April 1966. He was twenty-four!

As with Sonny Rollins's recordings at the Village Gate, a longer version of this record now exists, containing every recorded set from that week at that club. The version that lives in my body lasts about thirty-five minutes, whereas the longer version lasts for nearly five hours. So I have run with the long version, day after day, as I would with a long Theo Parrish DJ set, allowing for anything to happen. There are lots of repetitions, the sozzled MC Brisco Clark with the canned setup each night ("Are you ready for star time?") and his thank-you-for-coming-now-please-leave speech after the last song; Redding announces the presence of recording equipment over and over with the same joke—at first it's something about the louder you are, the more money we'll make off the recording, and therefore we can eat; but then the logic falls apart and you sense he's wondering why he even needs to make the announcement—"Yeah, we're recording an album right now, we're recording an album, so just holler as loud as you want! We gonna eat next week, we got to eat next week. Let your hair down, just holler loud as you want to, stomp hard as you want to, just take your shoes off, get soulful, you know? Just take your shoes on off, we'll get into a thing"—and finally he simply drops this part from the show. Redding had taken up the Rolling Stones song "(I Can't Get No) Satisfaction" about nine months earlier, and in his rendering it is not a complaint from a feckless creep but a pretext for joyful obliteration—he's communicating that he respects satisfaction and creates satisfaction and *is* satisfaction, and the origin point of the words doesn't particularly matter, so when you're into the second hour of this thing and the band starts another "(I Can't Get No) Satisfaction" and the first verse never arrives, it's just a vamp for ten minutes. "It's like staring into the sun," a friend of mine wrote about listening to Redding, a friend who has in fact taken up the same pilgrimage; we are walking the same Camino of this five-hour thing, and I'm noticing that Redding's singing can purify to such an extent that one's body seems to clarify while moving. James Brown might never show the limits of his physical capacity, but Redding finishes a song and he's short of breath, laughing. As a sound to have in your ears when you're running, the sound of someone gasping and laughing is nearly perfect: you become enthusiastic in your intentional disintegration on the road. By night two, the songs stretch out longer and longer. The need for an emphatic stop and rest seems to become artificial or academic, and when one runs to this music, its level of ongoing vitality can be helpful, not necessarily in terms of competitive stamina, but simply to help erase the boundaries between moving and stillness, to make that membrane as thin as possible.

Almost without exception, the structure of these songs in performance comes down to Otis Redding ascending to the top of a mountain, and then if not exactly easing down off the mountain for a denouement, then some sort of elongation of the apex, a relaxing of the ridiculous pressure he has put upon you, perhaps a realization that this is not a mountain at all but simply a higher ground level. When he reaches the higher level, he doesn't stop: he keeps going. He might move in circles; he might lie on his back and stare up at his own sun. As you get into day two and three of the three-day stand at the Whisky, you sense that Redding, in the manner of Keiji Haino, has now inhaled all the air in the club, and all the people in it, and he is now starting the massive exhalation. He's still breathing in, but the volume of air he expends, and the volume of air his horn players expend, slowly increases. And as Haino talked about wanting to make the air itself vibrate, you can hear something like this happen on Redding's Whisky recordings during the most intense soundings of the horn section: the sound seems to shimmer on the tape.

From the period when this music first entered my body, I remember the singing, the guitar playing, the drumming with great joy, but I remember the high-note trumpet player with bewilderment. In the constant heat of the extended moment, this trumpeter produced notes that went madly off track, that warbled and died in front of your ears; what was wrong with this man?

Not all music would accommodate the high-note trumpet player—only music that has enough greatness of soul. I am struck by the fact that this music could. And so I think about the out-of-place trumpeter finding his place within the gyre of the music as I run on the Otis Redding way, with no goal, no pretense of perfection at anything.

// 38 //

Thinking about breathing, the primary act I do as I run and the one I notice least, I've been rewatching a film on YouTube, made in 1991, of the hymn choir at the Mt. Do-Well Baptist Church in McConnells, South Carolina, singing "He Set Me Free." The bloc of choristers sits to the left of the altar, at a ninety-degree angle to the rest of the main congregation. Many of the singers, though not all, look to be over sixty. Many, though not all, are dressed in white. The cameraperson sits within the main congregation, turning the camera only slightly to take in specific members of the choir at one end or another. There aren't many of them—about fifteen.

They are not accompanied by a band or any rhythmic instrument. I'd say that the song begins, but language fails me here: neither "song" nor "begin" describes what happens. One member stands as casually as if he were stretching his legs or looking for someone in the church, and sings, distinctly but almost casually: "Well, he set me . . . free . . . ," and, at his own pace, he sits back down among the seated others. The rest of the choir joins in, repeating the line, though they all get to it by their own routes. Some stamp their feet in quarter notes, implying a slow procession. Some wait a little while to join, or perhaps join only by humming. Choristers lie back and look upward, or stare straight ahead, or bend down, but some smile, as if remembering something pretty; they are drawing power from not doing this uniformly. A few single notes at odds with the melody ring out to make the harmony thicker. Like Alice Coltrane falling into "Via Sivanandagar," they've begun, but the beginning seems assisted by nature or spirit, as if an unseen force were pushing it along. Better, perhaps, to say that the song is simply there, has been there, and they have discovered it, as one discovers a warm patch of sun or a sprinkler on a hot day, and they array themselves near it, at least to feel its mist, or to take a few turns running through the water.

> *I done been tempted and I done been tried.*
> *Jesus died on the cross*
> *just to set me free.*

This "He Set Me Free" includes verses—mostly a changeable line before two repeating ones, as well as a refrain—and a short melody, although I can't find evidence of the song as a published entity online. (It is not Albert Brumley's "He Set Me Free," copyrighted in 1939.) Perhaps it has no author. But what happens between and around the melody and the words matters more than whatever data I can provide to identify the song. The singers are familiar with the song, intimate with it, and open it up from many standpoints, some open-throated and some quiet, forming their own harmonies within understood boundaries, clapping and stomping for emphasis when they want to. The down-going countermelodies are as important as the up-going ones, and neither seem entirely necessary to the song or primary to its identity. After a full go-round of the verse, the elder who began the song chatters: "I won't stay that long, y'all. I just wanted you to know he set me free one day." A pause blooms while the stomping continues, but the song is in motion, so it can go in many directions now.

Sometimes living beings or natural forces can create a giant combination of breath, perhaps an antiphony and also a kind of free heterophony, the voicing of a primary line as well as its variants simultaneously; perhaps the identity of the main line shifts over time, and different forces sing different parts, on a slightly different schedule but in loose alignment, and together create an environment of chords or simply sound and intention in which it is hard to create a wrong note. Otis Redding did it with his group at the Whisky a Go Go, Pauline Oliveros proposed the possibility of it with "The Tuning Meditation," birds can do it in the woods, Aeolian harps can do it when played by the wind, the wind itself from various directions can do it. Some minutes into "He Set Me Free" a woman springs up, turns to look beside or behind her, and starts another verse as if to cheer the song on. The man who initiated the song sits in the corner, rather than leading the group by looking at them from a point position, and perhaps because he did start, he continues to come down especially hard on "Well, he set me," but most of the rest is done by felt agreement; as much as such a thing can be possible, the song invites and leads all of them. Six minutes in, the happening seems to end, or to fizzle out; there is no more singing, yet the stamping and clapping continue, but of course if there is no beginning as such, there is also no end, and this moment does not fizzle but rather opens into a complex passage of shuffling, throat-clearing, a few people continuing to stamp and murmur, until a choir member picks up a line from the song again. Nobody here is a virtuoso. A woman on the other end of the front row, younger than the other elders in the front, animates the song by tossing her head from side to side and moving her arms up and down in alternation. She puts her hands up in front of her, and sometimes she appears to be waving something away or bringing two hands down on a piano or massaging the horizon, moving freely to emphasize anything she hears. The group soars now: some members are clapping, some rise and start to dip and hop, keeping their outstretched hands down by their hips.

I learned of this video—though there are many like it—from a radio interview with the writer Ashon T. Crawley, whose book *Blackpentecostal Breath: The Aesthetics of Possibility* argues that such expressions in sound, or such breath-events in sound, have been either ignored or considered nuisances within the scope of European history and philosophy, at least since the Enlightenment. The fact that this version of "He Set Me Free" has no distinct beginning or end, and that shouting occurs, and that its leadership flows among members, combine to render it what Crawley calls "noise."

"The Blackpentecostal tradition does not make so much as it unmakes History," Crawley writes, "and an analysis of the noise, the joyful noise, emerging from varied spaces will elucidate such claims. Noise is the critique of the proper including proper History, proper historical memory, proper historical moment. Noise is that which is purported to *not* belong, that which supposedly waits in need of abatement."

Stepped in the water and the water was cold.
Jesus died on the cross
just to set me free

History, in this way of thinking, is a series of discrete material events that can be cataloged and related by someone in a position of power. Those events need to be kept separate, in order to be sellable as fixed narratives or melodies or lyric lines that can become properties. These material, copyrightable events must have a beginning and an end—a firm end, not a loose end—and they do need to have a single leader, if not a creator, if not a victor. If they can be ranked in order of importance, especially by artificial intelligence, even better, because all that really matters in this vision of History is the most important event, or the event that accrues the most power on Earth. This YouTube video isn't particularly easy to search for, and remains at best a partial representation of the song, the performances, such as they are, or perhaps only a symbol of them; you can't really get your hands around "He Set Me Free" by watching it, because everything about it has started before you got there and may not end till long after you're gone.

I haven't run to this music, because perhaps I hardly need to—it doesn't need me to activate it.

// 39 //

I've been relistening to a DJ mix by Theo Parrish called "ear-goggles," from 2021, a six-hour set done live over NTS Radio. I heard it, and then later Michaelangelo Matos wrote in his Substack that it might be the best DJ set he'd ever heard, making special mention of how Parrish used Fela Kuti's "Zombie," and I returned to it. I can't listen to it all in one run—perhaps someday, if I ever decide to try an ultramarathon—but I have listened to it in parts several times, over a number of runs. I like how widely Parrish stretches himself in the general task of putting the right thing on at the right time. I like engaging in the failed mission of assigning a narrative to the thing as a whole or in sections—it's a set, but would we call it "the work"? "The piece"? "The expression"? Perhaps it doesn't matter.

As I fall into running, then into its improvised routing—as I try all my tricks to move without reference to beginning or end—I notice how Parrish gradually breathes his set into being: he greets his listening audience on the microphone, then warms up, playing with words: "Am I tuned in? Are we tuned in? We tuned in together. Got some tunes. Tuning some tunes to keep tunes popping. Need tunes. . . ." Parrish lays a repeated vocal refrain by the singers on Michael White's "Journey of the Black Star"—"eee-ahh"—over the recorded voice of someone else entirely, who is setting up something else entirely, talking to a band: suggesting a beat, or speaking a beat into being. It's Jimi Hendrix, talking to his drummer, Buddy Miles, in the studio, three weeks after they performed "Machine Gun" at the Fillmore East. Hendrix is shuffling ideas around, making noise.

"Turn the drums up a little louder. . . . [indistinct] Where's the rest of that grass? Let's play with this. Start chak-a-toom, chak-a-toom. No, no, very old-time, only cymbal and snare." Here Hendrix imitates the famous "spang-a-lang" jazz-cymbal rhythm, which has no author. "Chak-a-toom. Chak-a-toom. Real old-time. No, no, not—that's too fancy. Yeah. OK, tell you what, do it without the snare. Start like that, OK? As soon as we come in, you come in with the bass drum and so forth. Huh? Hee-hee." And now Hendrix warms up, playing with words, playing with the voice of Elvis Presley at the beginning of "Trouble." "I feel evil," he croaks. He imitates Presley's breathless parlando: "If you've come for trouble, you've come to the right place." Then he imitates the opening lines of "Heartbreak Hotel," in full Presley quaver, before starting a different Presley song: "Blue Suede Shoes." "All right, one, two, three, go. . . ."

What Hendrix said in the indistinct moment, I later discovered, was "turn the drums up a little louder through the ear goggles." Parrish's source was a studio jam session included on a record sold outside the North American market four years after Hendrix's death, eventually titled *Loose Ends*, deemed unsalable in the United States and Canada by his record company, presumably for the reasons expressed by its title.

Hendrix fades out, and because of all the shuffling and the speaking-into-being of whatever Parrish's project is, we're off before we know we are off, into a piece of music by Ahmad Jamal. Sometimes one might know what or whom Parrish is playing, but often one doesn't know. Certain songs or voices or instrumental styles, virtuosic ones, ones that imply a special signature, the extremes or the corners of music, break through across this quarter day of almost entirely Black art—Jamal, D'Angelo, Erykah Badu, Madlib under the alias Lord Quas, Ray Barretto. But for the most part, if we were to try to devise a description for his mix, it's a long middle, put together by a cooperative mass. Sometimes it's a kind of antiphonal noise, never more so than when he includes his "ugly edit" of "Auf Wiedersehen, Darrio" by Dr. Buzzard's Original Savannah Band.

The jarring edit, the overlap, the extended form, is the noise of a DJ set. The roll is the noise of a striking foot. Breath is the noise of a note. Sweat is the noise of feeling heat.

The dance music in "eargoggles" keeps acknowledging jazz practice through echoes: much of it is funk played by musicians conversant in jazz; Lord Quas's recitation references dozens of performers in the jazz tradition, including ones played earlier in Parrish's set and ones mentioned in this book. And perhaps because the creation of a DJ set (or a song, or a book, or a run) often naturally involves a reprise, Parrish does perform a major one, it seems to me, by re-centering a previously stated theme.

At somewhere around the two-thirds point, Parrish plays "Vidgolia (Deaf, Dumb & Blind)," by Gil Scott-Heron and Brian Jackson, which joins several different instrumental sections within itself as well as several narrative points of view. One point of view is omniscient, or the free-indirect voice of Scott-Heron's conscience; one seems to be the voice of the exploitative American social structure, or the American system, speaking to its non-White citizens; a third seems to be a higher nihilistic power, maybe a devil figure, addressing the American social structure.

At any rate, referring to the Americans he elsewhere calls the "living dead," those who have been defeated by the system or who have made themselves willfully ignorant of it, Scott-Heron intones, "Zombie!" Ninety minutes later, near the end of his mix, after a stretch of Ray Barretto, Parrish cues up Kuti's "Zombie."

Both times that I have arrived at this part of the mix, the Kuti part, I have reached a kind of monument along the route, and run through various parts of the Bronx and Yonkers to get there. In the expanded present, I've entered the WPA stadium; run around its track; routed into the Parade Ground where it opens up at the southern end; turned onto the straight rail trail and taken it due north through the woods; passed another park, a swimming pool, a soccer field, and a golf course; passed the air-conditioning units behind a motel and a truck-rental place; run through several orders and styles of middle-class suburban housing; come out onto an arterial road and a light commercial strip that eventually becomes a former industrial district with flooring, heating, auto-detailing, and storage businesses, followed by a cemetery, toward working-class south-side Yonkers; run steeply up to Nodine Hill; and finally reached the water tower on Elm Street, fenced off with stern NO TRESPASSING signs, in a small memorial park. Nodine Hill is one of the poorest neighborhoods in Yonkers, very close to a much wealthier one, Park Hill; the income disparity here reminds me of Detroit, Parrish's city. The local papers write about the "Elm Street Corridor" in Nodine Hill as the place where the gangs are. Some low-level action hums around the bodegas; aside from that, on a bright morning there is nobody around, nobody but a runner.

The water tower holds a million gallons for the hill sections of the city. It stands on giant legs, a spider with a central post wrapped by a helical stairway, a vital resource, a stronghold, an alien tower, a protected municipal work in the middle of unfairness and scarcity. The writer Christina Sharpe has described her unreasonable fear of a specific water tower as a young person—I can see why. It could be a UFO, a Gigantor, a zombie. Before assuming its current spider shape, the tank stood within a 175-foot square brick column, which tipped over in 1938 when the interior tank buckled. "A wall of water—freighted with great chunks of brick and steel and iron railing—swept through the area," reported the Yonkers *Herald Statesman* the following day, "washing like lava down Elm Street and other immediate sections." It was a target too. A neighborhood historian online tells that the inhabitant of the house next door to the water tower was asked by "authorities" after 9/11 to report anyone taking pictures of the tank. It feels eerie to run by this tank, as one might run by a military encampment or dogs on chains—somehow risky to study it or look at it, and yet this is the way to register the unknown and the puzzling, practice your balance, continue to move, live in present and future together if at all possible, keep splicing.

Onward across the ball field on Nodine Hill, toward the grand old houses of Park Hill, down to the flatlands around Broadway, into the park again through the back end with its rocks and roots. Desiring silence and wanting to walk, I turn off the Parrish mix before it ends.

Bibliography

Music (in order of appearance)

Hendrix, Jimi. "Machine Gun," live at the Fillmore East, New York City, 12/31/69, second set, from *Songs for Groovy Children: The Fillmore East Concerts*. Sony Legacy, 2019. (The earlier one known to me was 1/1/70, first set, from *Band of Gypsys*. Capitol, 1970.)

Beethoven, Ludwig van. String Quartet no. 14 in C-sharp minor, Opus 131, performed by the Danish String Quartet, recorded 2017, from *Prism III*. ECM, 2021; also Budapest String Quartet, recorded 1940, from *The Complete String Quartets of Ludwig van Beethoven*. Columbia Masterworks, 1952; also Busch Quartet, recorded in 1936, from *Beethoven: The Late String Quartets*. EMI Classics, 2008.

Carter, Betty. "What a Little Moonlight Can Do," live at the Bottom Line, New York City, 1982, from *Whatever Happened to Love?* Bet-Car, 1982.

Subbulakshmi, M. S. "Bhavayami," from *Sri Venkatesa Suprabhatam*. His Master's Voice, 1963.

Cucina Povera. *Hilja*. Night School, 2018.

Nosebleed. *Nosebleed*. Grave Mistake, 2017.

DeVaughn, William. *Be Thankful for What You Got*. Roxbury, 1974. ("Hold On to Love," from reissued and updated album of the same name. Unidisc, 1994.)

Wonder, Stevie. *Songs in the Key of Life*. Motown, 1976.

The Beatles. *Beatles for Sale*. Parlophone, 1964.

Saint-Säens, Camille. *The Carnival of the Animals*. From Leonard Bernstein, with New York Philharmonic, *The Carnival of the Animals/The Young Person's Guide to the Orchestra*. Columbia Masterworks, 1962.

41 Original Hits from the Soundtrack of American Graffiti (film soundtrack). MCA, 1973.

Louis Armstrong and His Hot Five. *The Louis Armstrong Story Volume 1*. Columbia, 1956.

Davis, Miles. "So What," from *Kind of Blue*. Columbia, 1959.

Ohio Players. *Pleasure*. Westbound, 1972.

Toussaint, Allen. *Toussaint*. Scepter, 1970.

Dolphy, Eric. *At the Five Spot*, live at the Five Spot, New York City, 7/16/61. Prestige/New Jazz, 1961.

Cherry, Don, and Ed Blackwell. *El Corazón*. ECM, 1982.

Redman, Dewey, and Ed Blackwell. *Red and Black in Willisau*, recorded 8/31/80. Black Saint, 1985.

C.H.E.W. *Feeding Frenzy*. Iron Lung, 2018.

C.H.E.W./Penetrode. *Strange New Universe*. Neck Chop, 2017.

Ólafsson, Víkingur. *Debussy-Rameau*. Deutsche Grammophon, 2020.

Kuzan, Takahashi. *Take no Hibiki*, catalog number KT-1001. Label unknown, c. 1980s. Archived at Ben Gerstein's channel, youtube.com /@bengerstein.

Coltrane, Alice. *Huntington Ashram Monastery*. Impulse!, 1969.

Lockwood, Annea. *A Sound Map of the Danube*. Lovely Music, 2008.

Telemann, Georg Philipp. *Twelve Fantasias for Transverse Flute Without Bass*, performed by Barthold Kuijken. Accent, 1978.

Kanté, Mamadou. *Les Tambours Du Mali*. Playa Sound, 1994.

Jones, Bessie. *Get in Union*. Alan Lomax Archive, 2020 expanded reissue. (Also streaming tracks under "Bessie Jones 1961–1962." Archived at Lomax Digital Archive, archive.culturalequity.org.)

Sade. *Love Deluxe*. Epic, 1992.

Mal Waldron Trio. *Impressions*. Prestige/New Jazz, 1959.

Gubaidulina, Sofia. *Complete String Quartets*, performed by Stamic Quartet. Supraphon, 2012.

Halo, Laurel. *Public Knowledge: Carrier Bag of Music*. 2020. Archived at Laurel Halo's page, SoundCloud.

Kurtág, György, and Márta Kurtág. *Játékok*. ECM, 1997.

Kendricks, Eddie. *Eddie Kendricks*. Tamla, 1973.

Haydn, Joseph. String Quartets, Opus 20. Performed by the Chiaroscuro Quartet, from *Haydn: Quartets Op. 20, Nos. 1–3*. BIS, 2016.

Mayfield, Curtis. "Sun" *Beat-Club*, Bremen, Germany. Performed on 1/19/72. Archived at Beat-Club channel, youtube.com/@beatclub. "Curtis Mayfield Live at Beat-Club (1972.01.19), parts 1 and 2." Archived at facebook.com/sajukebox.

Parrish, Theo. *We Are All Georgeous Monsterss*. 2020. Archived at We are All Georgeous Monsterss channel, youtube.com/@weareall georgeousmonsterss5559.

Parrish, Theo. DJ set, live via Virtually Nowadays, 7/9/2020.

Giovanos, Alexandros. *Xenakis (Works for Percussion)*. Costa, 2022.

Parker, Charlie. *The Complete Savoy & Dial Master Takes*. Savoy Jazz, 2002.

Lustwerk, Galcher. *Information*. Ghostly International, 2019.

Bach, Johann Sebastian. Performed by Rachel Podger and Brecon Baroque, from *Bach: Double & Triple Concertos*. Channel Classics, 2013.

Astaire, Fred. *The Astaire Story*, recorded 1953. Verve, 1988 reissue.

Binchois, Gilles. Performed by Graindelavoix, *Joye: Les plaintes de Gilles de Bins dit Binchois*. Glossa, 2007.

Radigue, Éliane. *Jetsun Mila*, recorded 1986. Lovely Music, 2007.

Hope, Elmo. "B's A-Plenty," from *Elmo Hope Trio*. Contemporary, 1959.

Thelonious Monk Quartet. *Monk's Dream*. Columbia, 1963.

Rodríguez, Arsenio. "La Gente del Bronx," recorded 1953, from *Cómo se goza en El Barrio*. Tumbao Cuban Classics (reissue), 1992; "El Elemento del Bronx," recorded 1966, from *Viva Arsenio!* Bang, 1966.

Ice Spice. *Like..?* 10K Projects, 2023.

Dry Cleaning. "Dry Cleaning Live from Bandcamp HQ." 2022. Archived at Dry Cleaning channel, youtube.com/@drycleaningband.

Burkina Faso: Volume 1. Sublime Frequencies, 2021.

Sonny Rollins Quartet with Don Cherry. *Complete Live at the Village Gate 1962*, recorded live at the Village Gate, New York City, 7/27/62– 7/30/62. Solar, 2015.

Redding, Otis. *Live at the Whisky a Go Go: The Complete Recordings*, live at the Whisky a Go Go, Los Angeles, 5/8/66–5/10/66. Stax, 2016.

Mt. Do-Well Baptist Church hymn choir. "He Set Me Free," filmed by RAM at Mt. Do-Well Baptist Church, McConnells, South Carolina. Archived at Hymn Choir channel, youtube.com/@Hymnchoir.

Parrish, Theo. "Theo Parrish Presents eargoggles (6 Hour Mix)—NTS 10" live via NTS Radio, 4/23/21. Archived at nts.live.

Words

Alsadir, Nuar. *Animal Joy: A Book of Laughter and Resuscitation*. Minneapolis: Graywolf Press, 2022.

Bacon, Francis. Interviewed by David Sylvester, in Sylvester, *Interviews with Francis Bacon*. London: Thames & Hudson, 2016.

Barthes, Roland. "The Grain of the Voice," in *Image, Music, Text*, translated by Stephen Heath. New York: Hill and Wang, 1978.

Barthes, Roland. "Listening," in *The Responsibility of Forms: Critical Essays on Music, Art, and Representation*, translated by Richard Howard. New York: Hill and Wang, 1985.

Beatty, Paul. *The Sellout*. New York: Farrar, Straus and Giroux, 2015.

Berger, John. "Field." *New Society*, vol. 18, issue 475, 1971.

Berger, John. "Some Notes on Song: The Rhythms of Listening." *Harper's Magazine*, February 2015.

Bickford, Susan. *The Dissonance of Democracy: Listening, Conflict, and Citizenship*. Ithaca, NY: Cornell University Press, 1996.

Cage, John. "45′ for a Speaker," in *Silence: Lectures and Writings*. Middletown, CT: Wesleyan University Press, 1961.

Caramanica, Jon. "Ice Spice Broke Out with 'Munch.' Rap's New Princess Is Just Warming Up." *New York Times*, January 20, 2023.

Chaudhuri, Amit. *Finding the Raga: An Improvisation on Indian Music*. New York: New York Review Books, 2020.

Chaudhuri, Amit. "Storytelling and Forgetfulness." *Los Angeles Review of Books*, September 20, 2019. I am indebted to this essay particularly for some of the thinking in chapter 30, and in a general way for the thinking in many other places.

Coen, Ray. Interviewed by David García, April 26, 2000. Archived at Bronx County Historical Society website.

Cregan-Reid, Vybarr. *Footnotes: How Running Makes Us Human*. New York: St. Martin's Press, 2016.

Crews, Harry. Interviewed by Rob Michaels, in "Harry Crews: Pen-Packin' Old Boy." *Motorbooty*, vol. 5, Winter 1990.

Croce, Arlene. *The Fred Astaire & Ginger Rogers Book*. New York: Outerbridge & Lazard, 1972.

Davey, Moyra. "The Problem of Reading," in *Index Cards*. New York: New Directions, 2020.

Decker, Todd. *Music Makes Me: Fred Astaire and Jazz*. Oakland: University of California Press, 2011.

Dostoyevsky, Fyodor. *The Brothers Karamazov*, translated by Richard Pevear and Larissa Volokhonsky. New York: Everyman's Library, 1992.

Erpenbeck, Jenny. *Go, Went, Gone*, translated by Susan Bernofsky. New York: New Directions, 2017.

Fosse, Jon, *Septology I–VII*, translated by Damion Searls. Oakland: Transit Books, 2022.

Freeman, Lindsey A. *Running*. Durham, NC: Duke University Press, 2023.

Fuyo, Hisamatsu. "The Hitori Mondo of Hisamatsu Fuyo" (self-interview), translated by Robin Hartshorne and Kazuaki Tanahashi. From the International Shakuhachi Society website: https://www.komuso.com/people/people.pl?person=105.

García, David F. *Arsenio Rodríguez and the Transnational Flows of Latin Popular Music*. Philadelphia: Temple University Press, 2006.

Gonzalez, Evelyn. *The Bronx*. New York: Columbia University Press, 2004.

Haino, Kenji. Interviewed by Alan Cummings, in *Halana*, 7/29/1996. Archived at halana.com.

Hammons, David. Interviewed by Kellie Jones, in *Art Papers*, July/ August 1988.

Hershorn, Tad. *Norman Granz: The Man Who Used Jazz for Justice.* Berkeley: University of California Press, 2011.

Holiday, Harmony. "The Sound of Black Voices, The Sound of my Father." *Literary Hub*, June 15, 2018.

Hurston, Zora Neale. "Shouting" and "How It Feels to Be Colored Me," in *Folklore, Memoirs, & Other Writings*. New York: Library of America, 1995.

jazz, jennifer. *Spill Ink on It.* New York: Spuyten Duyvil Publishing, 2020.

Jenkins, Stephen. *The Story of The Bronx: From the Purchase Made by the Dutch from the Indians in 1639 to the Present Day*. New York: G. P. Putnam's Sons, 1912.

John Milner Associates, Inc. *Van Cortlandt Park Parade Ground Phase 1A Archeoilogical Investigation Borough of the Bronx, New York*. Prepared for Abel Bainnson & Butz and the New York City Department of Parks & Recreation, November, 2007. Retrieved at http://s-media .nyc.gov/agencies/lpc/arch_reports/1029.pdf.

Jones, Bessie, and Bess Lomax Hawes. *Step It Down: Games, Plays, Songs, and Stories from the Afro-American Heritage*. New York: Harper & Row, 1972.

Kelley, Robin D. G. *Thelonious Monk: The Life and Times of an American Original*. New York: Free Press, 2009.

Kelly, Ellsworth. "Fragmentation and the Single Form," in *Ellsworth Kelly: Fragmentation and the Single Form*, June 15–September 4, 1990, Museum of Modern Art. Archived at moma.org.

Kramer, Lawrence. *The Hum of the World: A Philosophy of Listening*. Berkeley: University of California Press, 2019. Kramer's idea of "the audiable" is referenced with attribution in chapter 34, but in chapter 1, I am influenced in a general way by his use of the word "hearken" and his thoughts about the visual versus the aural.

Lee, Riley Kelly. *Yearning for the Bell: A Study of Transmission in the Shakuhachi Honkyoku Tradition*. Doctoral thesis, University of Sydney, 1992.

Lees, Gene. *Oscar Peterson: The Will to Swing*. Toronto: Lester & Orpen Dennys, 1988.

Le Guin, Ursula K. *The Carrier Bag Theory of Fiction*. London: Ignota, 2019.

Madden, David, and Jeffrey J. Folks, eds. *Remembering James Agee*. Athens, GA: University of Georgia Press, 1997.

Mathieu, W. A. *The Shrine Thief*. Cambridge, MA: Terra Nova Press, 2024.

Matos, Michaelangelo. "BC001—Theo Parrish on NTS Radio, April 2021–July 2022." *Beat Connection*, September 9, 2022. https://michaelangelo.substack.com/p/bc001-theo-parrish-on-nts-radio-april.

Mayfield, Todd, with Travis Atria. *Traveling Soul: The Life of Curtis Mayfield*. Chicago: Chicago Review Press, 2016.

Menzies-Pike, Catriona. *The Long Run: A Memoir of Loss and Life in Motion*. New York: Crown, 2016.

Merleau-Ponty, Maurice. *Signs*, translated by Richard C. McCleary. Evanston, IL: Northwestern University Press, 1964.

Molleson, Kate. "Occam Ocean: In Search of Sound Within Sound," from *Sound Within Sound: Radical Composers of the Twentieth Century*. New York: Abrams, 2022.

Morales, Ed. "75 Years Ago, Latin Jazz Was Born. Its Offspring Are Going Strong." *New York Times*, January 10, 2023.

Murakami, Haruki. *What I Talk About When I Talk About Running*. New York: Alfred A. Knopf, 2008.

Naison, Mark, and Bob Gumbs. *Before the Fires: An Oral History of African American Life in the Bronx from the 1930s to the 1960s*. New York: Fordham University Press, 2016.

Neal, Larry. Review of Pharaoh Sanders's *Karma*, from *The Cricket*, issue 4, 1969; republished in *The Cricket: Black Music in Evolution, 1968–69*. New York: Blank Forms, 2022.

Ong, Walter J. *Orality and Literacy: The Technologizing of the Word*. London: Methuen, 1982. I am particularly influenced by Ong's notion that "sight isolates, sound incorporates."

Online Etymology Dictionary, etymonline.com, written and compiled by Douglas R. Harper.

Ono, Seigen. Interviewed by Shuta Hasunuma. "Shibuya Soundscape: Listening to the Footsteps of Shibuya." *Tokion*, July 28, 2020.

Paine, Thomas. *The Age of Reason*. London: J. Watson, 1851.

Rainer, Yvonne. *Feelings Are Facts: A Life*. Cambridge, MA: MIT Press, 2013.

Ratliff, Ben. *Coltrane: The Story of a Sound*. New York: Farrar, Straus and Giroux, 2007.

Sillitoe, Alan. *The Loneliness of the Long-Distance Runner*. London: W. H. Allen, 1959.

Sontag, Susan. "The Aesthetics of Silence," in *Styles of Radical Will*. New York: Farrar, Straus and Giroux, 1969.

Stockfelt, Ola. "Adequate Modes of Listening," in *Audio Culture: Readings in Modern Music*, edited by Christoph Cox and Daniel Warner. London: Bloomsbury, 2017. Stockfelt uses the term "dishearkening," which I have used in chapter 2; he defines it as "to refuse to listen," but I am thinking more along the lines of listening while not-listening, or perhaps just hearing.

Storch Associates. *Van Cortlandt Park, Borough of the Bronx: Restoration Master Plan for the City of New York Department of Parks and Recreation*, report, 1986.

Szwed, John F. *Alan Lomax: The Man Who Recorded the World*. New York: Viking, 2010.

Terry, Peter C., Costas I. Karageorghis, Alessandra Mecozzi Saha, and Shaun D'Auria. "Effects of synchronous music on treadmill running among elite triathletes," *Journal of Science and Medicine in Sport*, vol. 15, no. 1, January 15, 2012.

Waldron, Mal. Interviewed by Ted Panken, WKCR, February 25, 2002. Archived in transcribed form at tedpanken.wordpress.com/category/mal-waldron.

Washburne, Christopher. "The Clave of Jazz: A Caribbean Contribution to the Rhythmic Foundation of an African-American Music," *Black Music Research Journal*, vol. 17, no. 1, spring 1997.

Weil, Simone. "Human Personality," from *Simone Weil: An Anthology*, edited by Siân Miles. London: Virago, 1986.

Whitman, Walt. *Complete Poetry and Selected Prose and Letters*, edited by Emory Holloway. London: Nonesuch Press, 1938.

Wilde, Oscar. *The Critic as Artist*. New York: David Zwirner Books, 2019.

Wilmer, Valerie. *As Serious as Your Life: The Story of the New Jazz*. Westport, CT: Lawrence Hill Books, 1977.

Films, TV, images, video, and audio interviews

Audubon, John James. *Roseate Tern*, mixed-media watercolor painting, 26⅛ × 20¼, 1832. Archived at https://www.audubon.org.

Berger, John. *About Time*. 1985. Archived at youtube.com/@gerryco2317.

Enzensberger, Hans Magnus. "Second Thoughts on Consistency," James Lecture for the New York Institute for the Humanities, 1981. Archived at nyihumanities.org/the-vault.

Ichikawa, Kon, dir. *Tokyo Olympiad*. 1965.

Lockwood, Annea. Interviewed by Arie Altena. Sonic Acts XIII, 2010. Archived at Sonic Acts' page on Vimeo: https://vimeo.com/12692600.

Lomax, Alan, and Forrestine Paulay, dirs. *Dance and Human History*, as seen in excerpts in Robert Gardner's conversation with Alan Lomax, August 1975, on *Screening Room*. https://video.alexanderstreet.com/watch/alan-lomax-conversation-with-robert-gardner-from-the-screening-room.

Loveless, Stephanie, and Brady Marks. "Soundwalk Generator." furiousgreencloud.com.

Mili, Gjon, dir. *Jammin' the Blues*. 1944.

Schjeldahl, Peter. "The Critic as Artist, in 2011: Updating Oscar Wilde." International Association of Art Critics/USA Distinguished Lecture, 2011. Archived at Vera List Center's page on Vimeo: https://vimeo.com/33271180.

Thank you:

Amit Chaudhuri, Rachel Kaadzi Ghansah, Harmony Holiday, Karen Holmberg, Kim Kashkashian, Yvonne Kendall, Margaret Hiatt, Bob Ludwig, Michaelangelo Matos, Laura Monti, Eddie Palmieri, Nicole Sin Quee, Jonathan Rhoads, Bettina Richards, who are in it, in one way or another.

Nik Cohn, W. A. Mathieu, Chris Richards, and Sam Stephenson, who also read it.

The students in the Age of Listening and Criticism's Possible Futures writing classes at NYU Gallatin, 2016–2024.

Yves Beauvais, Nat Chediak, Kwami Coleman, John Colpitts, Vybarr Cregan-Reid, Robert Fanuzzi, Mark Feeney, B. G. Firmani, Sharon Gray, Mike Hamad, Arto Lindsay, Julie Malnig, Daniel Nosonowitz, Piotr Orlov, Carla Parisi, Dr. Steven Payne of the Bronx County Historical Society, Amanda Weintraub Ratliff, Marcus Ratliff, Emma Reynolds, Hanson Reynolds, Jake Reynolds, Linda Reynolds, Peter Reynolds, Rachel Reynolds, Gio Russonello, Rob Saffer, Parul Sehgal, Alex Star, John Szwed, David Terrien, Leron Thomas, Jim White.

My agent, Zoë Pagnamenta. At Graywolf, my editor, Ethan Nosowsky, as well as Katie Dublinski, Caitlin Van Dusen, Marisa Atkinson, Nirali Sheth.

For my wife, Kate Reynolds, and my sons, Henry Ratliff and Toby Reynolds. And my father, Marcus Ratliff, 1935–2022.

BEN RATLIFF is the author of books on music including *Every Song Ever: Twenty Ways to Listen in an Age of Musical Plenty* (Farrar, Straus and Giroux, 2016) and *Coltrane: The Story of a Sound* (Farrar, Straus and Giroux, 2007). He was a pop and jazz critic at the *New York Times* from 1996 to 2016, and has written for other publications, including the *New York Review of Books*, the *Washington Post*, and *Presence*. He teaches at New York University's Gallatin School of Individualized Study and lives in the Bronx, New York.

Graywolf Press publishes risk-taking, visionary writers who transform culture through literature. As a nonprofit organization, Graywolf relies on the generous support of its donors to bring books like this one into the world.

This publication is made possible, in part, by the voters of Minnesota through a Minnesota State Arts Board Operating Support grant, thanks to a legislative appropriation from the arts and cultural heritage fund. Significant support has also been provided by other generous contributions from foundations, corporations, and individuals. To these supporters we offer our heartfelt thanks.

To learn more about Graywolf's books and authors
or make a tax-deductible donation, please visit
www.graywolfpress.org.

The text of *Run the Song* is set in Freight Text Pro.
Book design by Rachel Holscher.
Composition by Bookmobile Design & Digital
Publisher Services, Minneapolis, Minnesota.
Manufactured by Versa Press on acid-free,
30 percent postconsumer wastepaper.